Jonny Muir is an adventurer, runner, writer and proponent of UK-inspired travel. Born in Birmingham in 1981, he grew up and was educated in north Worcestershire, before studying history at the University of Exeter. Family holidays in south-west England, the Peak District, Wales and Scotland kindled a life-long love affair with his home nation.

Jonny visited the UK's 91 historic county tops in a continuous 5000-mile cycling and walking adventure over a three-month period in 2006. His first book, *Heights of Madness*, published in 2009, is an account of that unique journey. He is also the author of a guidebook, *The UK's County Tops: Reaching the Top of 91 Historic Counties*.

A journalist for six years at newspapers in Cheltenham, Peterborough and Inverness, he subsequently retrained as an English teacher, and now works at a secondary school in London.

By the same author

Heights of Madness
The UK's County Tops

ISLES AT THE EDGE OF THE SEA

Jonny Muir

SANDSTONEPRESS
HIGHLAND | SCOTLAND

Reprinted 2011

First published in Great Britain by
Sandstone Press Ltd
PO Box 5725
One High Street
Dingwall
Ross-shire
IV15 9WJ
Scotland.

www.sandstonepress.com

Editor: Moira Forsyth

The publisher acknowledges subsidy from
Creative Scotland towards publication of this volume.

ISBN: 978-1-905207-61-9

The paper used in this book promotes sustainable forest
management and is PEFC credited material.

PEFC

Cover design by River Design, Edinburgh.
Typeset by Iolaire Typesetting, Newtonmore.
Martins the Printers, Berwick upon Tweed.

Contents

⊕

Acknowledgements

I would not be writing these words were it not for the faith placed in me by my publisher, Sandstone Press. Thank you to the publishing team, notably Moira Forsyth, my editor. The joy of travel is in the people one encounters: the crotchety bus drivers, the round-the-world cyclists, the roomful of snoring strangers, the walker who stood next to me on Conachair, the ceilidh crowd on Eigg, the marshals on the windy summits of the Paps of Jura, the 'whisky brothers', the Barra tourist who bought me a cup of tea, the English sailors who filled my glass. It is the littlest gestures that live longest in the memory.

I have, however, some specific thanks: to the volunteers at the Centre for World Peace and Health on Holy Island, for persuading me not to 'ceaselessly strive'; to Fiona Hogg, for fixing my right knee; to Magnus Houston, for keeping his promise to get me up the Inaccessible Pinnacle; to George Broderick, for his expert insight on Gaelic and the Paps of Jura fell race; to Kenny Macleod, for welcoming me into his church and home; to Anna MacArthur, for educating me on the nuances of the Free Church of Scotland; to Dougie and Karen MacDonald, for rescuing me in my hour of need on Skye; to my parents, Lynda and Roger Muir, for their unshakeable support; and, of course, to Fi, for putting up with not only my prolonged absences, but the endless hours of writing. She

Acknowledgements

cannot have minded too much; she agreed to be my wife.

Finally, to the Highlands and islands of Scotland: the most beautiful, challenging and extraordinary places on our planet. I may be hundreds of miles away in London, but to unashamedly borrow a pair of lines from the chorus of *Caledonia*: 'Let me tell you that I love you, that I think about you all the time.'

List of Illustrations

List of Illustrations

Maps

☙

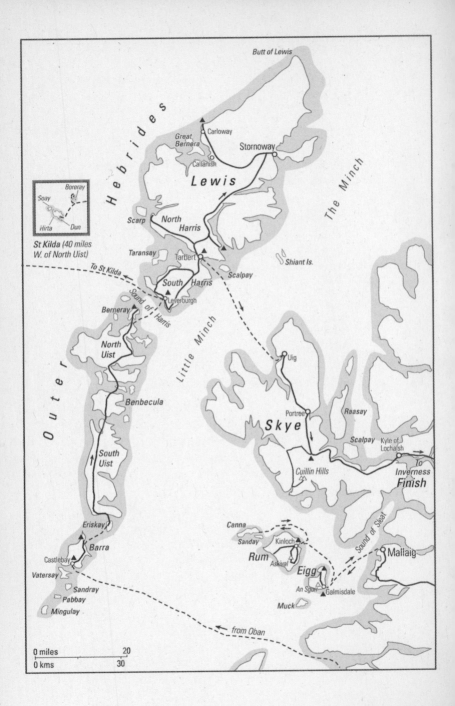

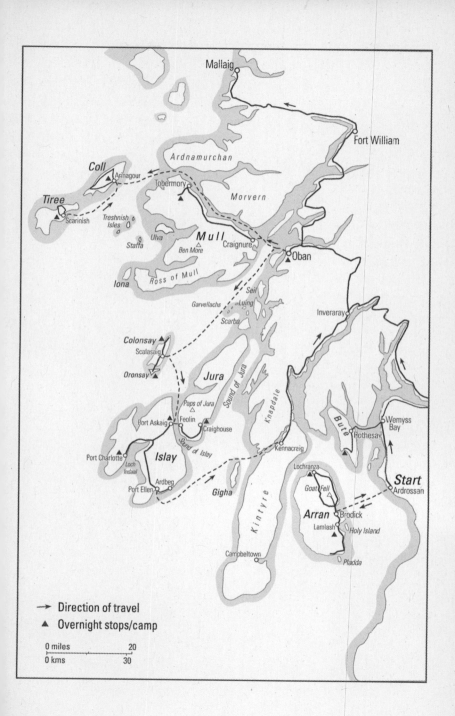

Nowheresville

O Caledonia! stern and wild,
Meet nurse for a poetic child!
Land of brown heath and shaggy wood,
Land of the mountain and the flood,
Land of my sires! what mortal hand
Can e'er untie the filial band
That knits me to thy rugged strand!

Sir Walter Scott

&

Meteorologist Tomasz Schafernaker was partway through a live Saturday afternoon bulletin on BBC One when he casually waved a hand over the hundreds of wondrously-shaped islands pitched off the west coast of Scotland.

He pronounced rain. Nothing unusual in that. Except these were the words Schafernaker uttered thereafter: 'This lumpy stuff you can see here, these clouds have actually been producing a few showers, but it's mainly in the Western Isles, mainly in nowheresville, and it looks as though the east of Scotland will keep the sunshine.'

Nowheresville: a place void of identity, charmless and undistinguished.

It was an unfortunate choice of word.

Schafernaker did not forecast the subsequent cloudburst: a media storm, a tempestuous one of his own conjuring. Angus MacNeil, MP for the Western Isles, was unimpressed. Nor were his constituents enamoured; one

1

islander branded the comment 'insulting, ignorant and self-satisfied'. The BBC received a 'squall of complaints', the *Times* punned.

Schafernaker's crime? He had reduced the Hebrides – a place of faultless natural beauty with flowering machair meadows, towering mountains and white-sand beaches washed by cobalt seas; a place of inimitable spirit, the birthplace of Christianity in Scotland and the source of the globe's most revered single-malt whisky; with St Kilda, *the* island at the edge of the world, a cultural and physical marvel, in a league with Ayers Rock and Machu Picchu, among its isles – to nowheresville.

It was like calling Elle Macpherson ugly. Or water fattening. Or the Earth flat.

Schafernaker said sorry – after identifying Scotland's north-west hinterland as nowheresville for a second time during a later broadcast on the BBC news channel. He had been misconstrued, Schafernaker said in an apology: 'My intention was only to convey that very few people were likely to catch a shower on that day. It was in no way a comment or opinion on the area or the people that live there.' Nowheresville, the forecaster explained, was meant to refer to the mountains of the Highlands, not the islands of the Hebrides. That makes it all right then.

Deciding not to be offended, Scottish author Jenny Colgan, writing in the *Guardian*, offered a fresh slant: 'Now, let me see – if Schafernaker lives in London and works in television, it's a near-certainty he lives in Notting Hill or Shepherd's Bush. Hideous traffic, litter-strewn streets, the congestion charge, bendy buses and £5 cappuccinos? Now that's what I call nowheresville.'

1

Arran

Arran I would call on the whole the most delightful; more enjoyable even than Skye, partly because smaller, though scarcely less wild, but chiefly because of the better condition of its inhabitants.

Sheriff Alexander Nicolson

⚭

'Number 68.'

I was being summoned to the start line of the Goatfell hill race – eight miles of toil from sea level in Brodick to the 874-metre pinnacle of Arran, and back again: the sort of thing perfectly sane people do for amusement.

'Yes, me,' I muttered, reluctantly walking forward to join the other competitors, a throng of lithe, sinewy men and women wearing little more than club singlets and shorts. I stole an anxious upwards glance at the skyscraper we would soon be climbing. The imposing impression of Goatfell glowered back, turning my legs to lead. I dreaded the next minutes of my life; they would involve certain pain.

Only nature could have engineered such an accomplishment, but were Goatfell a building, it would be the tallest in the world, standing 46 metres above the ludicrously-lofty, 160-storey Burj Khalifa in Dubai. Imagine the staircase in that high-rise. If a flight of stairs to the summit of Goatfell existed, the number of steps would exceed 4000 – an extraordinary figure. Not only must the Goatfell runner ascend the equivalent of many thousands of steps, they must descend them too. There is a further complication. No two of these 8000 steps is the same: they are an ever-changing variety of big and small, short and long, loose and firm, dry and wet, flat and sloping, smooth and rough, grassy and rocky, hard and soft.

Hill running is not meant to be easy.

The herd was released. Some 80 bodies surged forward in unison, first bustling around a playing field, then spilling onto Arran's round-island road and turning north. Goatfell loomed above us, its summit – our destination – touching the heavens, seemingly a lifetime away. I lowered my eyes, focusing my gaze on the road ahead, mentally preparing for the battle to come. The race route swept us away from Brodick and across Glenrosa Water, with a marshal directing the pack of runners onto a minor road. I was soon on the lower reaches of the mountain, ascending a rocky uneven track through forest.

The adrenaline of the start had gone. Banter and blether had fizzled out. I had not been running uphill long, but already I was conscious of overwhelming tiredness, a profound weariness in my legs. I fought the desperate urge to simply stop, to cease movement. A foot hurt, then a thigh, then the other foot, then a hip, and so it went on. The hill runner's enemy, lactic acid, engulfed both calves. I contemplated walking. At least then I would still be moving. Too soon, far too soon, I resolved, scolding myself.

Lacking the will to confront pain, I succumbed, slowing to a depressing shuffle, then – inexorably – an undignified walk. The rhythm of running broken, the psychological fight had been tamely fought and easily lost. The roof of Goatfell, now almost directly above my head, seemed further away than ever; there was still a CN Tower and two St Paul's cathedrals to go.

I continued up Goatfell, following a track that climbed

unbroken to Meall Breac, a stony ridge leading to the mountain's summit, half-running, half-walking. I tried to recall why I had thought it would be a sensible idea to spend the first day of my journey among the west coast islands of Scotland racing up a mountain. If there had ever been logic in the madness, I could not recall it now. The path became rougher, littered with boulders and jagged rocks. To compound my frustration, I was being overtaken. After sneaking into the top-10, I had been unceremoniously spat out of the elite. A runner silently skipped past me, then another, and another. More would follow.

Climbing towards the sun, I developed a maddening thirst and fantasised about what I would drink later to quench it. Then I began to panic. I was due to take part in the Isle of Jura fell race in a fortnight, a contest twice as long and involving three times the ascent of Goatfell. I asked myself the same question over and over again in my head: if I struggle on Goatfell, how will I fare on Jura? It was not as if Goatfell was reputed for its extreme toughness. The race is not even the hardest on Arran. The Glen Rosa horseshoe, a 12-mile dash over Goatfell and neighbouring Cir Mhòr, took that accolade. Then – in the context of the Scottish islands – there was the Glamaig race on Skye, a tortuous contest up and down a cone of scree that a bare-footed Ghurkha once completed in less than an hour; the 'Mull monsterette' over Ben More, the highest mountain on Mull; and, of course, the race over the formidable Paps of Jura. In the hill running stakes, Goatfell was a kitten among lions.

There was no let-up, the terrain became steeper and steeper. There was still a Canary Wharf to ascend. I hauled myself skywards, dragging my aching body across heather, grass, mud and rock. The track was increasingly ill-defined, a rough route through a maze of rocks and across loose soil. I was wallowing in my hellish existence when I looked up to see a runner hurtling downhill towards me. It was the race leader, a man who had already been to the top and was on his way back to Brodick. Surging downhill with apparent reckless abandon, he looked like a man who had just been told his house was on fire.

Just when it seemed I might be climbing forever, the land before me abruptly flattened, and there it was: a miracle – the rocky crest of Goatfell. I stumbled towards a marshal positioned by the summit toposcope, snatching a fleeting glance across the island I had conquered. The prize was glorious: an unending panorama of islands, mountains and ocean.

The spell-binding landscape of the British Isles takes on an extra echelon of greatness when viewed from the Goatfell zenith. Writing in 1628, the Scottish traveller William Lithgow described Arran as being 'sur-clouded with Goatfieldhill which with wide eyes overlooked the western continent, and the northern country of Ireland; bringing also into sight in a clear summer's day, the Isle of Man and the higher coast of Cumberland. A larger prospect no mountain in the world can show, pointing out three Kingdoms at one sight.'

When Sheriff Alexander Nicolson, a late-19th century pioneer of climbing in Scotland, stood here, his eyes were drawn to the surrounding mountains and their interlinking ridges. 'The two chief features of it that impress one in succession are, first the terrible congregation of jagged mountain ridges and fantastic peaks right opposite and very near you, with their shelving precipices and dark clefts and wild melancholy scaurs,' he recalled.

I did not have time to saviour the spectacle. But in the moment of that fleeting glance, my spirits soared. This was where I belonged: running up a mountain, a free, striving spirit, pushing myself to mental and physical limits, always putting one foot in front of the other. Exhaustion, frustration, self-doubt and thirst vanished in a puff of exultation.

The epiphany was short-lived. I had to descend the 4000-step staircase. This is the moment when hill running can seem a rather pointless exercise. What is the sense in stretching every sinew to reach the highest point in the shortest time, only to retreat to the lowlands as soon as the task has been accomplished? I have never liked descending. I am too sensible, incapable of switching off dark thoughts of blood and broken bones. The previous year's race had been a bloody event and I did not want to be the unlucky one in the back of an ambulance. Disengage your brain, hill runners urge one another. To me, disengaging my brain on a running descent of Goatfell was tantamount to disengaging my life. So I tiptoed down cautiously, petrified of falling, agonising over every step. A group of four runners drifted past me, stretching their lead to hundreds of metres in the space of two minutes. Be brave, be bold, I told myself, but it was not until the gradient had softened that I began to stretch my legs, to run as fast as I could run without fear.

A man standing to the side of the path was telling runners their positions. I was 20th. Moments after imparting the information, he articulated a far more enthusiastic cry: 'First woman.' They are the words many a male runner dreads: misplaced masculine pride the reason, not sexism. The utterance lit a spark of desperately-needed motivation. I ran hard and fast until I could no longer hear the woman's footsteps behind me. I had dropped her. Back on the road, the finish line still more than a mile away, I did not slacken, furiously passing three of the four runners who had overtaken me on the descent. I crossed the line in 17th place, a polite ripple of applause greeting my return to sun-drenched Brodick.

Lolling on the playing field several minutes later, mug of tea in one hand, block of shortbread in the other, my jumbled emotions settled into one feeling: thank goodness that is over – a notch above 'never again'. But memories of pain and suffering are brief. An hour later, sitting in a beer garden outside the Ormidale Hotel, alcohol now in the hand that had held tea, I convinced myself that I had actually taken pleasure in running up and down Goatfell. Paps of Jura, I thought – a doddle.

When I was a boy I would draw islands, miniature worlds of my own creation. Putting a pencil to a blank sheet of paper, I would start with the outline – sometimes fjord-like and serrated, sometimes smooth and sweeping. I would sketch a narrow, isolated peninsula, at the end of which would be a jumble of treacherous rocks and a lighthouse built high above a crashing sea. Not all ships had heeded the warning beam. A ship, lying abandoned and askew, had been wrecked on the stony maw of the rocks. Picking up my colouring pencils, I would add detail to the coastline.

The shore would be attired with sand, shingle and seaweed, broken by tremendous cliffs and rolling meadows, secluded coves and broad bays. I would draw white waves breaking on the beaches, while in other places the water would be calm and still. The interior would feature fearsome, stupendous, snow-capped mountains, perhaps a volcano spewing magma. There would be a lagoon or a lake, with an island in the middle – an island within an island. And what else? Dense forests, a pier, villages, footpaths along cliff tops, a castle, a river growing wider as it neared the sea, a dam, a pack of wild animals. The possibilities were endless – it was my kingdom, after all. Offshore would be sandbanks and sailing boats, dorsal fins and flying fish. Seabirds in the shape of an upside down 'w' would soar overhead. At the top of the picture would be a large, glowing, yellow sun.

I had three months of island-hopping ahead of me, four if I wanted, and no itinerary. That was the way I wanted it. Travel is not travel when it is contrived. I had one fixed notion: to journey overland and overseas in a generally northerly and westerly direction until I had reached the St Kilda archipelago, the farthest, remotest outpost of the British Isles, a Utopia gone wrong. The year was 2010; it was 80 years since the last remaining inhabitants of St Kilda – notorious for its seabird-eating population – were evacuated from their faraway island. To get there, I would cycle, run and walk, as well as thumbing the occasional lift. I would travel on boats and buses, and become accustomed to the inter-island ferries of Caledonian MacBrayne (or Cal Mac, as the firm is commonly known).

A desire to visit the islands of the west, not in a series of weekend or even week-long excursions, but as part of a long, unbroken journey, was a slow-burner. The idea, a romantic dream, had crystallised in my mind in the un-romantic environs of a first-floor office occupying an Inverness business park. There I spent 18 months working for the Highland and Inverness editions of the *Press and Journal*, editing and writing stories about the islands: un-certainty surrounding air services to Barra; the growing environmental credentials of Eigg; the campaign to make Harris Scotland's third national park; bitter Presbyterian opposition to Sabbath sailings from Lewis; sea eagles on Mull; a community buyout on Rum; plans to celebrate the 80th anniversary of the evacuation of St Kilda.

At times, however, I felt like a fraud. I had never seen these places, never set foot on them. How could I write about somewhere I had never visited, somewhere I had very little knowledge or understanding of? I imagined readers in Castlebay, Stornoway or Tobermory laughing at the efforts I, an Englishman, made to unravel their concerns, their lives, their ways. Even my geography was uncertain. I would need to consult a map to establish the correct position of Islay in relation to Jura, or double check I had not inadvertently called the Small Isles the Summer Isles.

I quit, telling my colleagues I was leaving to explore the islands. I told my housemate I was moving out. I invested my savings in a mortgage, buying a flat with my girlfriend Fi in London. Seeking life after journalism, I gained a place on a teacher-training course.

But London and teaching were months away. The summer was my own.

It was late when Fi called. Rescuing my phone from the depths of my sleeping bag, I whispered into the receiver so as not to wake the other campers on the Glen Rosa site I had made home. Parting had not been easy. We had moved into our flat in early-April, busying ourselves with cleaning and decorating, putting our own stamp on the property. My imminent departure was rarely discussed. A month and a week rolled past until it was mid-May and time to go.

'How long will you be?' she had asked.

'I don't know, as long as it takes,' I said, snapping back.

Perhaps I should not have gone at all, resisted the temptation of my island affair? My itinerant streak had already put a strain on our relationship, ultimately destroying it – albeit temporarily. We spent a year apart, 'a gap year' we called it, Fi in London, I in Inverness. And now, given a second chance, here we were again, with me disappearing for an unspecified period of time – the very factor that drove a wedge between us. I had often wondered how one balanced a desire to explore the world with the love for another person. I decided it was not possible to give your heart to both, certainly not at the same time.

There is a joke about an Englishman, an Irishman and a Scotsman going on a mountain-climbing expedition. They become trapped on the peak, but a fairy appears offering to transform them into birds so they can escape the narrow ledge they are poised on. The Englishman chooses a swan, the Scotsman a golden eagle. As is often the case, the Irishman is the butt of the joke. He chooses a penguin. Arran has its own version of the Englishman, Irishman, Scotsman yarn, except in this case there is no Irishman and the punch line is a grisly variant. The tale goes something like this: an Englishman and a Scotsman went on a mountain-climbing expedition in the dark, granite peaks of Arran, but only one returned. The other was murdered – or so it seemed.

The death of Englishman Edwin Rose, apparently at the hands of Scotsman John Laurie in 1889, is believed to be the only case of murder in the British mountains to come before a court. Rose's body was discovered beneath a stone-built shelter on the south side of Glen Sannox, three weeks after the pair had set out for a walk on Goatfell. The death of Rose was a brutal one. His skull had been smashed into eight or nine pieces and his spine, a shoulder and ribs were broken. Laurie went on the run for two months before being arrested in Hamilton. After an unsuccessful attempt to take his own life, he insisted: 'I robbed the man, but I did not murder him.'

The Coatbridge pattern-maker was tried and found guilty at Edinburgh Crown Court by a majority of one in a 15-strong jury which deliberated for only 45 minutes. Laurie's decision to steal some of Rose's possessions, flee Arran, and evade arrest pointed to his guilt, the prosecution argued.

But the evidence against him was circumstantial only. No blood or murder weapon was found on Laurie, nor could any eyewitness place the supposed assassin at the 'murder' site. Upon being sentenced, Laurie turned to the benches in the courtroom and declared: 'Ladies and gentlemen, I am innocent of this charge.' He continued to plead his innocence until his death 40 years later in 1930.

I hoisted my bulging rucksack onto my shoulders, the weight, supplemented by litres of water, almost causing my legs to buckle beneath me. Looking at a map of Arran earlier, reaching Lochranza by late-afternoon had seemed a realistic proposition. My route would take me up Glen Rosa, over two mountaintops – Cir Mhòr and Caisteall Abhail, from where I would be able to see the site of Rose's death – before a long descent to the north coast.

Yet with the unexpected strain of the load and the tiredness of a fell race in my legs, a 10-mile excursion to Lochranza no longer seemed rational. The prospect was downright absurd. I could have caught a bus instead. Even so, I soldiered on; I wanted to see where Rose came to a macabre end.

Arriving at a junction, I was faced with a choice between a low and a high road. The low road would see me continue on the gently-rising track that ran along the floor of Glen Rosa. The high road veered west, climbing up and up, and crossing two ridge-linked mountains. Low or high, the destination – Cir Mhòr – would be the same, although the high road was unquestionably the way of the mountain masochist. Foolishly, I chose the hard way, climbing steeply and sweating profusely. The weather was much worse higher up. Rain soon began to fall. There was no shelter. The terrain was boggy, the path indistinct. I had made the wrong choice. I turned back, descending to Glen Rosa.

Frustrated at the energy exerted and the time wasted, I marched up the glen towards the toothed triangle of Cir Mhòr. My pace dawdled as I laboured towards The Saddle, a narrow plateau of land between the 799 metre mountain and Goatfell. It was close to this point that Rose had been pushed or, if the account of Laurie is to be believed, where Rose fell. The walkers had only met three days earlier at a hotel on Bute and sailed to Arran the following day. Laurie and Rose spent the latter's final hours climbing with two others, before the group split, leaving the infamous pair to ascend Goatfell. They were seen on friendly terms on the summit by five witnesses. In a letter to the *North British Daily Mail*, Laurie claimed he left Rose 'in the company of two men who came from Lochranza and were going to Brodick after summiting Goatfell'. The only certainty is that Rose – either alone, with Laurie or with the two mystery walkers – fell to his doom from a point midway between the peaks of North Goatfell and Mullach Buidhe.

I could not fathom how Cir Mhòr could be surmounted. I stared up at the mountain's seemingly impenetrable maze of buttresses and cliffs from The Saddle for some time before I spied four figures far above ascending the peak by way of a thin track. I followed them. The climb was arduous and unyielding, made doubly difficult by the bricks I seemed to be carrying on my back. At one point I had to clamber through a gap between two rocks, then haul myself up to a third. For a moment I lost my grip; I was detached from the mountain. My weight thrown backwards, I had a brief, fearful sensation of falling, before I clawed at a rock and regained my balance.

Now high above The Saddle, the path weaved across the northern face of Cir Mhòr, passing tremendous buttresses, before squirming its way to a pointy summit. A whistling wind was frantic in its attempts to force me from this plinth, but as I crouched in the shelter of a boulder, the revelation of seeing sea all around was a joyous reminder that I was an islander. I had almost forgotten I was occupying such a territory, so engrossed I had been in mountains, murder and the wild interior of Arran.

Beyond the snow-filled corrie of Beinn Tarsuinn, the majesty of Goatfell and the sweeping glens of Rosa and Sannox, I could see Arran's place in the world. There was the long arm of Kintyre to the west, with Gigha beyond, while to the east the islands of Bute, Great and Little Cumbrae, and Holy Island, interrupted the Firth of Clyde.

Not long after I was standing on a second summit. Despite rising to a greater altitude, the tor-littered top of Caisteall Abhail lacked the grandeur of Cir Mhòr. But from here I was able to look across Glen Sannox to Coire nam Fuaran, the place where Rose's face-down body was discovered by a search party. Only a fortunate man would survive a drop from such a place, regardless of whether the fall was accidental or not. Men have died in lesser tumbles. The Londoner would not have been able to halt his plunge. His head would have been repeatedly dashed on rocks. Was Rose pushed? Was Laurie the victim of a gross miscarriage of justice? We will never know. The mystery belongs to the mountains.

Looking north I experienced a smidgen of what Ernest Shackleton and his two companions on the ill-fated Endurance expedition must have felt when they glimpsed civilisation on the south Atlantic island of South Georgia in 1916, for there was Lochranza, my salvation. The comments uttered by Frank Worsley also came to mind as a warning: 'Boss, it looks too good to be true.' Though visible at last, Lochranza sat a long way off, still several hours away.

I descended on a path that followed the curve of a cliff-edge, only for the track to peter out. Plunging downhill,

I began an exhausting slog across a terrain of wobbling boulders and gorse. Going down was worse than going up. My legs, smarting from the application of Goatfell, throbbed with every step. I longed to reach the path marked on my map, but when I did it was as bad as tramping over rough country had been: more loose, ankle-twisting rocks and stretches of sopping bog.

The terrain at last began to ease, the path growing drier and more distinct. I turned a final corner and a distillery and houses appeared, now minutes away, not hours. Soon I was walking on a road, my feet grateful of a firm, flat surface after seven hours of unevenness. I was dirty, drained and disgruntled when I clumped into the youth hostel at Lochranza.

At least I had managed to walk out of the hills. Edwin Rose had not been so lucky.

2

Holy Island

May every wonderful and wholesome thing arise here on
Holy Isle and may its goodness and happiness spread
throughout the entire world.

Lama Yeshe Rinpoche

⬩

Of all the days to cancel a ferry.

Dawning bright, the morning had grown luxuriously
sunny. It was balmy: shirts and shorts weather. As I consumed a bacon and egg brunch at a café in Lamlash, the
prospect of the weather possibly foiling my expedition
across the mile-and-a-half strip of sheltered water to Holy
Island was unfathomable.

Then as I approached the ticket office at the edge of the
pier, there it was, the unthinkable reality, scribbled in black
and white: 'No sailings due to wind forecast.' It was
blustery, admittedly, and winds of up to 40mph were
anticipated, but right now the sea appeared at ease, calm
and flat. It was a glorious day. I walked the length of the
pier, stopping at the end and peering down at the clear
water below, then raising my eyes to Holy Island.

Two miles long and half-a-mile broad, the island rose
from the shimmering waters of the Firth of Clyde like a
possession of a fairytale. The three nations of Britain each
have a Holy Island and this is Scotland's. The spiritual
heritage of Holy Island dates back to the 6th century, when
a miracle-performing Christian saint named Molaise took

16

up residence in a cave above the tide line on the west coast. A monastery was built on Holy Island in the 13th century and the island was Arran's chief burial ground up to the 1780s. The burials ceased after a boat carrying mourners capsized, with up to eight people drowned. Today, apart from a pair of lighthouses, the outpost has two other prominent buildings: the Centre for World Health and Peace, garnished by an arc of ornamental stupas running from a stone jetty to the front of the white building, to the north; and the Inner Light Retreat, where at least a dozen women were soon to begin a four-year retreat, shutting themselves off from the world beyond the island's rocky fringe, to the south.

Lama Yeshe Losal Rinpoche, the Tibetan abbot of the Samye Ling Monastery in Dumfries and Galloway, who first visited Holy Island on the winter solstice in 1990, found the place reminded him of a vision seen while practising dream yoga in the US in the early 1980s. After raising a vastly reduced asking price of £350,000, the island was signed over to Lama Yeshe by the then owners, James and Kay Morris, in 1992. Mrs Morris, a staunch Catholic, said she has been instructed by the Virgin Mary in a dream to pass Holy Island on to Lama Yeshe.

The first one-year retreat was held at the Inner Light Retreat in 1995; the 65-bed Centre for World Peace and Health, offering courses on harmony and happiness, aimed at 'finding calm in our busy and stressful lives', opened in 2004. The centre and the island are not exclusive, however. Its facilities are open to Buddhists and non-Buddhists, even those with no faith. But Tibetan Buddhism is a key component of life on Holy Island, with the isle's 253 hectares dedicated to 'nurturing spirituality and exploring the deeper meaning of life'.

All who come, either for a day trip or a course, must

abide – or are asked to abide – by the island's five 'golden rules', based on the five precepts of Buddhism: to protect all life and refrain from killing; to respect other's property and refrain from stealing; to speak truthfully and refrain from lying; to encourage health and refrain from all intoxicants (including alcohol, cigarettes and drugs); to respect others and refrain from sexual misconduct.

There would be no chance of finding my inner peace today. The weather – or, more accurately, the forecast – had seen to that. Stuck as I was on Arran, at least I was in good company. The Dalai Lama attempted to visit Holy Island in 1993, but his also intended excursion was abandoned due to the wayward Scottish weather.

I caught a bus destined for Kildonan, a small community perched on the southern rim of Arran, overlooking the island of Pladda. Four university students – three Sassenachs and an Arranach – were already on board, each with their backs to a window and legs stretched across seats. The Arranach had invited his friends to visit his home island and was revelling in the role of tour guide. As the bus rolled through Lamlash, the most gregarious of the Englishmen listed the village's landmarks aloud as we passed them, the tone of his voice gaining in incredulity at each one.

'A Co-op . . . a church . . . a butcher . . . a high school!'

The latter he uttered with astonishment. O brave new world that has such amenities in it. As if Arran – Scotland's seventh largest island and home to some 5000 people – could possibly need a high school?

'Nice place to visit, but I couldn't live here. Where would you party?' another Sassenach mused, as he gazed across Lamlash Bay to Holy Island. 'That's a cheeky house over there, mind you,' he said, pointing to the Inner Light Retreat.

'That's a monastery,' the Arranach corrected, 'monks live there.' Which was almost right.

The conversation was typical student fodder – who had had sex with whom, who had nearly had sex with whom, and the physical merits of their respective mothers.

'Mate, I just think your mum's fit,' one of the group apologised to another.

As the bus climbed above Dippin Head, dome-like Ailsa Craig, a 338-metre high island off the Ayrshire coast where granite is quarried to make curling stones, loomed on the horizon.

'Look at that little booby,' one of the quartet called out, pointing in the direction of Ailsa Craig.

Little booby? It seemed a tad unfair. If Ailsa Craig must be likened to a breast, surely it would be a large one?

'Also known as Paddy's Milestone,' the Arranach chipped in, maintaining his responsibility as tourist guide.

From breasts and islands, the conversation took a twist, with butchering becoming the new topic of discussion.

'All these cows,' the Lamlash list-maker said, gesticulating towards fields of grazing cattle with murder in mind, 'and only one butcher. Let's start a butcher? We would make a killing.' He laughed. 'A killing – get it?'

I had been watching another of the passengers – a little, elderly woman, erect and lively, sitting immediately behind the students. She shifted uneasily in her seat and on a couple of occasions seemed on the verge of saying something, only to think better of it a moment later. Then she could stand it no longer. Her raspy voice cut through idle exchanges. There was obviously more than one butcher on Arran, she announced, so, no, your butchery services are not required here. And now, will you please – for all our sakes – shut up?

Or words to that effect.

The bus was silenced.

I wandered across an expanse of windswept, golden sand at Kildonan, and finding a large rock to shelter behind I sunbathed for a while. There was little to see of Pladda, a mile offshore; the island was green and low-lying (its name means flat isle), and the only building was a lighthouse.

Back in Lamlash, I ran for the first time since my Goatfell excursion but my legs were stiff and unwilling at first. A rough path led north along the coast to Corriegills, then dog-legged inland, climbing to Dun Fionn, the site of an Iron Age hill fort overlooking the firth and Holy Island. I continued across the forested Clauchland Hills, conquering its 260-metre high point and seeing only a dog walker, before plunging downhill to Lamlash. Dinner, cooked outside my tent door, was a messy affair: leftover pasta, half-cooked beans and sausages (the gas ran out), day-old hummus, bread and chocolate. The fine weather had passed. The clouds were now dark and heavy with rain. The wind whipped incessantly at my tent. Now this was proper ferry-cancelling weather.

The enchanting Holy Island of yesterday had vanished overnight. The isle was now eerie and stern, the sea grey, and Mullach Mòr, the 314-metre summit, swaddled in mist. Even so, the ferry boat was running, and a 10-minute journey in drizzle across Lamlash Bay brought our nine-strong group to a jetty on Holy Island. The water beneath us had become Scotland's first 'no take zone' in 2008. No marine life can be removed from this northern third of Lamlash Bay by any method, either commercially or re-creationally. The rest of the bay was a 'marine protected area', where only a limited amount of fishing was permitted. The intention is two-fold: to preserve the banks of maerl (a pretty, pink, coral-like seaweed) at the northern entrance of the bay, and to bolster the populations of queen scallops, cod and pollock, which it is hoped will in time spill over into neighbouring waters where there are no restrictions on fishing.

One of the volunteers at the Centre for World Peace and Health met us on the pier. Introducing himself as Kenny, he delivered a pithy introduction to the island: the history of the centre, the significance of the women-only Inner Light Retreat, walking routes along the coast and up and over Mullach Mòr, and the resident wildlife (130 Soay sheep, 30 Eriskay ponies and 25 Saanen goats).

'Any questions?' he asked.

'What are the women being treated for?' a mishearing American tourist queried.

I followed Kenny along a path named Happiness Avenue, according to a finger post, that led through a herb and vegetable garden to the entrance of the centre.

'Don't think people are rude if they don't talk to you,' he said quietly. 'They are on a silent retreat, 10 days.'

Kenny told me to wait at the reception, before popping his head around the door a minute later, asking: 'Hungry?' He thrust a bowl of sausages (vegetarian, naturally), mashed potatoes and onion gravy into my hand. As we retraced our steps through the garden, a Carmelite nun, wearing brown robes and her head bowed, crossed our path.

We continued to the island's information centre, known as the boathouse, and sat around a large, wooden table. Between forkfuls of food, Kenny, a 40-year-old Glaswegian, told me he had travelled across India and been employed as a builder before beginning work as a volunteer on Holy Island a year ago.

He was in a reflective mood. 'I feel very present here,' Kenny explained. 'The island gives me a lot of space to think, and I have a lot more control over my thoughts and my life.' I sensed he was motivated by something far deeper, something unspoken, that he was not prepared to reveal.

We were joined by Adam, originally from London and a full-time volunteer on the island since 2006, who concurred. 'The island is like a TARDIS, giving you space to learn about yourself,' he said, nodding at Kenny.

I pressed them, finding the statements bland and vague, wishy-washy even. What made Adam, a man in his 40s, give up his girlfriend, his job, his life, to work for nothing as a rhododendron basher on a largely unknown island in the Firth of Clyde, and then decide to stay indefinitely?

'This isn't just about escaping the rat race is it? There's got to be more to it than that,' I implored.

Adam tried to explain. People are 'ceaselessly striving', he said. They possess a never-ending ambition, impacting on their health and wellbeing. The identity of these people is created by the culture they immerse themselves in – their friends, their job, the music they listen to, the films they watch. Holy Island had given him the opportunity to strip his life back, to discover his inner peace, to find the real, unadulterated person within, not some soulless creation of society.

'And Holy Island is also a very beautiful place, a really pretty place, and I meet lots of interesting people. Nearly everyone who comes here experiences a strong, powerful energy. People feel safe here.' He became serious again. 'People need to stop. It's as simple as that. But most people in the western world would find it hard to stop.'

Adam and Kenny were among a group of 15 unpaid volunteers who ran the Centre for World Peace and Health. They are not tied to the island, coming and going as they wish, visiting family and friends on Arran and the mainland on their days off. They have access to books, films and the internet, unlike the guests they look after.

More volunteers piled into the boathouse; they were preparing for a birthday party that night. Final touches were made to a decorative cardboard cut-out, which would be used for a game of pin the tail on the Eriskay pony.

The 60 bed centre, with a 100 seat conference hall, runs a year-round programme of courses, from creative writing and meditation to tai chi and yoga. Lama Yeshe would himself visit the island to lead a 'compassion retreat' in the late summer. The clientele are predominately Christian or secular, often middle-aged women, and a third are regulars. They come from all over the world: Australia, South Africa and the US, seeking personal development. Courses generally last a weekend, a fortnight at most, with retreats held over Christmas and Hogmanay. The 35 people at the centre on the day of my visit were on a Vipassana retreat, a traditional Buddhist meditation. For some of these visitors, like Adam, the experience of Holy Island would be life-changing.

I walked down the line of the eight stupas, Tibetan prayer flags between each one. Found at locations of religious significance, the four sides of the square base of the stupa represent the qualities of mind needed to attain enlightenment: love, compassion, joy and equanimity. A vertical signpost, with the words, 'may peace prevail on Earth', had been erected by the stupa closest to the shore. I had seen an identical sign in Dulwich Park in London.

Passing through a gap in a stone wall, I picked up a path, quickly gaining height as I climbed in a curve above the centre. Small signs saying 'this way please' and 'to the top' guided me across the peaty slopes of Mullach Beag, the lower of Holy Island's two hills. A pair of ponies were mooching close to the eastern shore, oblivious to my presence. I descended to a bealach between the peaks, before ascending sharply to the island's summit, now free of cloud. A trig pillar on the grassy, steep-sided high point was decorated with a tangle of prayer flags, a collection of coins, from pennies and pounds to cents and euros, and seashells.

The drop to the south side of the island was sheerer than the climb from the north, with the Inner Light Retreat and Pillar Rock lighthouse being revealed as I lost altitude. I passed a group of six Dutch women, visiting Holy Island as part of a walking holiday on the islands. One of the walkers was scared of heights. Perverse but brave, I thought, that the vertigo-sufferer should attempt a hill scarcely higher than any land in the Netherlands.

I stopped at the gate of the Inner Light Retreat. A sign read: 'No entry. Retreat in progress.' A retreat was not in progress, but its commencement was imminent. A four-year cloistered retreat of up to 15 women was due to begin in the autumn, while 21 men would start another retreat at a centre on Arran, with the two vigils running simultaneously. The women, some who have made life vows as nuns, are likely to have shaved their hair as a 'token of renouncing attachment'. They will not dress up, wear make-up or jewellery during the retreat. They will be celibate and teetotal. They will have no direct contact with the outside world: no newspapers, radio, television or telephone, although visiting lamas will inform them of matters of global significance, such as natural disasters or terrorist attacks. Letters to and from family and friends are permitted, but only 'on a monthly basis'.

The purpose of the retreat? According to Chokyi Lhamo, leader of the first traditional three-year and three-month retreat on the island, which ended in 2006: 'To dismantle the armour of protective devices built up over years and lifetimes to cope with life situations, and experience the mind in its simple state with no pretence, nothing to prove, just to be as we are.'

And the purpose of the four-year length of the retreat? 'A long retreat allows the mind to settle away from the distractions and busyness of usual concerns, and in the process gain clarity and insight. The individuals who choose to do such a long retreat usually do so because they wish to go deeper within, and that takes time.'

A path now clung to the western shoreline, passing depictions of the Buddha and Tibetan saints painted onto rocks. Soay sheep, introduced to Holy Island in 1970, flitted about the beach, balancing nimbly on rocks. The island's Saanen goats stayed away from the coast, preferring to graze on grassland to the east of the Inner Light Retreat. These curious horned beasts have lived here for 700 years, having been brought to Holy Island by the Vikings, despite the breed originating from Switzerland. The upturned shape of their mouths gave the appearance of a fixed, disconcerting grin.

Midway between the Inner Light Retreat and the Centre for World Peace and Health, I came to a 'healing spring'. Like the trig pillar on Mullach Mòr, the spring – traditionally thought to cure ailments and bless those who drink the water – was adorned with coins, flowers and shells. A ladle lay across the gifts, waiting to be plunged into the clear water. A sign does not specifically tell people not to drink the water, merely pointing out that the spring does not meet 'current EU drinking water quality standards'. I weighed up the options: the opportunity to be blessed and healed, or concede to a bureaucratic decree over something that was likely to be perfectly drinkable? I scooped my hands into the shape of a bowl, thirstily slurping the water. Above the spring was the hermitage of St Molaise, who chose to live here – a cave beneath an overhanging sandstone rock – rather than accept the throne of Ulster.

The ferry whisked us back to Arran. The afternoon had

slipped by too fast. I had felt at peace. I had not, alas, located my inner peace. That would be unthinkable in only four hours on Holy Island. Even the men and women on the four-year retreats may not find true spiritual enlightenment.

But as the boat swept across the smooth water of Lamlash Bay, I promised to heed Adam's words, and as such, I left the island with my soul a little lighter.

3

Bute

Camping: the art of getting closer to nature while getting farther away from the nearest cold beverage, hot shower and flush toilet.

Unknown

꩜

Irrational fears keep us young. When I no longer have these incongruous, unfounded terrors, my life will surely not be worth living. Bute was not a fearful place. There were no poisonous plants, no man-eating animals, no mass murderers on the loose. Yet, as I lay alone and timid in my little tent, senses razor-sharp, I had become convinced my life was in peril.

I had probably never been safer. Such are the absurdities of irrational fears.

Waking on Arran, I came to Bute later that morning, rising early and catching a bus to Brodick, a ferry to Ardrossan, and a further bus to Wemyss Bay. The dull outlines of Bute and its neighbours Great and Little Cumbrae were hazily visible through mist as I travelled north along the Ayrshire coast. The fog thickened, obscuring the Firth of Clyde trio.

The Bute-destined ferry was a floating old people's home, packed with doddering gangs of coach parties from the mainland. Rothesay gradually appeared through the murk. There is a line in the traditional Scottish tune, *Song of the Clyde*, which goes: 'Then Scotland's Madeira that's Rothesay, they say.' The town's apparent likeness to the Portuguese archipelago is by virtue of its palm trees and its mild climate. Tourism-reliant Rothesay was no Madeira today. Its Victorian buildings were grand and impressive when viewed from the sea, but on land Rothesay was dilapidated and rundown.

The soubriquet of Bute as the unexplored isle is also a misnomer. Its position at the northern end of the Firth of Clyde makes it one of the most accessible of Scottish islands to Glasgow, and home to more than 7000 people, twice as many as Mull. With little over an hour-and-a-half of travelling time separating Bute and Glasgow, people can feasibly work in the city, commuting to and from the island each day. At least that is how Bute is marketed. One of the strap-lines of Bute Gateway, a partnership established to boost economic regeneration on Bute, reads 'island but not isolated'.

My inter-island via mainland journey had imbued in me a sensation of jetlag. I slunk into a café on the Rothesay seafront and ordered a bacon sandwich. I sat staring at a wall, only conscious of the sound of a radio, the station it was tuned to playing the songs *Reach for the Stars*, *The Bonnie Banks o' Loch Lomond* and *Eye of the Tiger* consecutively. I doubted that any station had ever or would ever again play such a gloriously haphazard compilation of songs in the same order. It was a moment of history.

Mount Stuart, the family seat of the Stuarts of Bute, direct descendants of King Robert the Bruce, seemed the obvious place to go. It was either there or the Victorian Toilets in Rothesay. The bus followed a seashore-hugging road and passed the English-inspired hamlet of Kerrycroy, before cutting inland to Mount Stuart, where a dozen of us were dropped outside an ultra-modern visitor centre made of glass and wood. I meandered through wooded gardens, part of the 120 hectares of land which surround Mount Stuart, with the red sandstone house appearing at the end of a tunnel of trees. The coach parties had beaten me to it; several vehicles were parked single-file on the road outside Mount Stuart, the drivers huddled together smoking cigarettes.

Known for its fantastical Victorian Gothic architecture, the existing house was created by the third Marquess of Bute and his architect, Sir Robert Rowand Anderson, in the late-19th century, after the previous house burned down in 1877. With its Italian marble staircases and pillars, giant tapestries, zodiac windows, paintings of British royalty and caged tweeting canaries, I thought of Mount Stuart as the antithesis of Holy Island: egotistical, grand and lavish, yet captivating in its splendour. When the 3rd Marquess died in 1900, his obituary in the *Herald* described his home as 'one of the most magnificent specimens of domestic architecture in existence'.

I went back to Rothesay, back to the café, this time noticing the name – Café Zavaroni. The name and its significance to Bute rang a faint bell. Then it dawned on me – Zavaroni, as in Lena Zavaroni, the child singer who grew up in Rothesay and died aged 35 after battling anorexia for two decades. Discovered in 1973 by holidaying record producer Tommy Scott, Lena appeared on *Opportunity Knocks* later that year, topping the viewers' vote for five consecutive weeks with her version of *Ma, He's Making Eyes At Me*. The song reached number eight in the music charts and she appeared on *Top of the Pops*, the youngest singer ever to do so. Lena was aged just 10. Success followed success: she was dubbed the next Barbra

Streisand, performed sell out concerts at the London Palladium, sang at the White House for President Gerald Ford and appeared on the *Morecambe and Wise Show*. But the singer was battling well-documented demons, suffering from a serious eating disorder from the age of 13, and later depression. Lena had undergone neurosurgery that was hoped would finally cure her anorexia when she died of pneumonia three weeks later in 1999.

Café Zavaroni is run by Lena's cousin, Margaret, who is also reputed to have a fine singing voice. She was an affable host, endearing and honest. Margaret was happy to hear Lena's name mentioned by customers, with memories of her cousin's life stirred by news that a biopic, *Going Nowhere: The Lena Zavaroni Story*, was to be made. I told Margaret I was planning to wild camp on Stravanan Bay on the west of the island.

'Watch out for the cows,' Margaret had confusingly called out from the kitchen as I left.

I took another bus to the south, disembarking at Kingarth, from where a mile-long road walk brought me to the start of a track dropping to the sea. I went the wrong way, traipsing through a stinking farmyard and coming to a cul-de-sac, with the mournful gaze of a herd of cows scrutinising my every move. Back on the right path, I passed between fields of cows and sheep, with the view ahead of straggly gorse and a dull sea. Low dunes, but no fence (now I understood why Margaret had warned me about cattle), separated the grazing land from the beach, a half-mile stretch of grey sand. Apart from the occasional squawking of a seabird, there was no sound. The air was still and breathless; the mist remained, dim and dirty.

Legalised in 2005, wild, informal camping – basically, pitching a tent anywhere outside the confines of a designated site – is permitted in Scotland (although not in England and Wales) provided the camper remains a discreet distance from homes and roads. The rewards of living beneath canvas cannot be reaped until a camper has escaped the prosaic and sterile environment of an organised site. People ensconced in such places might indeed be sleeping in a tent, but they are not truly camping. My alternative accommodation tonight was at a site where my neighbours would have undoubtedly been a row of static caravans – the ugliest sight known to man.

The joys of wild camping are boundless: re-connecting with nature, sleeping beneath the stars, breaking out from the electronic world of computers, mobile phones and televisions. As romantic as that sounds, camping rough has the same snag as camping at an organised location: if (and, in all likelihood, when) it rains, living can be truly awful. The outdoors life suddenly becomes the indoors life, and the indoors of a tent are ridiculously small.

For all its charms and idealistic allure, wild camping is, however, fraught with complexities. When I told Margaret about my intentions to sleep in Mother Nature's bosom, she raised an inquiring eyebrow. Do not lone people camping in remote places tend to get bludgeoned to death by a psychopathic fugitive? That only happens in the US or in films, and certainly not on Bute, I assured her.

Her reaction was typical: 'I would never do that.' Her response is what many people utter at the prospect of digressing outside the perceived safe haven of a camping ground. That is if the concept of sleeping on the ground, under canvas, in the cold, can be stomached in the first place.

The more a person camps wild, the more accustomed and savvy to the outdoor world – the night time outdoor world in particular – they inevitably become. A greatly enhanced sense of danger, invoked by overactive imaginations, can usually be kept in check as experience grows. The first-time wild camper must overcome these anxieties. Human nature is to go with the crowd. Being a loner is seen as unconventional, an emotional flaw in a person's character. Humans are so unused to being on their own that when we walk away from the masses, the sudden sense of being alone, of isolation, is deeply unnerving. It generates a guilty sense of unease, as if something is being done that should not be done, and at any moment there is the possibility of being found out.

I was not a first-timer, nor was I wild camping veteran. Irrational fears remained. The axeman had always been the imagined physical realisation of my fears. It started out as a joke, a mild source of amusement. A friend and I slept overnight at Red Point bothy, a former youth hostel overlooking Loch Torridon and a three-mile walk from the end of the road at Diabaig. An axe and a saw hung on an inside wall opposite the front door. As it was a bothy, the door stayed unlocked; anyone could come and go. As night fell and as the only occupants, the presence of these weapons of mass destruction caused us both an unspoken anxiety. It was more than spooky. I was scared. The tools were for chopping wood. What else would they be used for? But as I lay my head on a pillow that night, all I could think of was that a phantom axeman (not a saw-man, for some reason) was coming to chop us up into little pieces.

The worst thing about being in a tent if the axeman did come calling would be a chronic inability to defend myself, since my penknife could offer only scant opposition. Imagine hearing a rumpus outside your tent: a raised voice, threats of the axing variety, that sort of thing. Lying prostrate, half-asleep and semi-clad in a contraption that cannot be seen out of is not an ideal starting place to begin a defence of one's life.

My favourite wild camping story is told by round-the-world walker Karl Bushby in his book *Giant Steps*. Bushby was camping in Argentina, a little different to Bute, I acknowledge, when he was approached by a man asking if he was alone.

'He gestured as to whether there was room in my sleeping bag,' Bushby wrote. 'No, I must have got it wrong . . . surely this wasn't what he was asking? I hoped he'd piss off. He then asked for some toilet roll and disappeared for, I assumed, a crap, only to return and sit down in front of me with his trousers round his ankles. Well, I was gobsmacked. Before I knew, he turned round and stuck his bare arse into my tent and pointed at my crotch. He soon got the picture and fled in his car.'

At least such an episode had yet to happen to me.

Wild camping can also be a logistical nightmare. In order to cook, clean and drink – provided these things are important to the camper – water must be carried in, and water is annoyingly heavy. It is easier in the mountains, where water can be siphoned from streams. The lowlands are a different story; I could never trust the hygiene of a burn that was running off farmland. The rotting carcass of a sheep could be lying unseen in the water a few yards upstream. Nor do I know what chemicals the land may have been treated with and subsequently runoff into the water supply. There is a great deal of water to be found in the sea. Unfortunately, it tastes bloody awful. As well as water, food must be lugged in too, for the essence of wild camping is that a café or shop will not be close at hand, and even if they were, they would almost certainly be closed by 5pm. This is Scotland, remember.

And then it comes to the moment of choosing the actual

piece of ground to pitch the tent, the time, for me, of endless procrastination. This is no specifically-designed camping and caravan site; scant few places are flat, free of rocks, near a stream, sheltered, hidden from homes – all the things needed to fulfil the obligation to be a responsible guest yet also guarantee comfort. I spent the best part of an hour traipsing across the sand, grass and dunes of Stravanan Bay in search of the optimum pitch. Is it level? Can I be seen from the farmhouse? Am I too close to a golf course? In the end, I pitched my tent next to the fence of the course, in full view of the farmhouse, two other homes and 100 or so cows, and on uneven ground above the beach. With the tent finally up, a three course dinner followed – bread, pasta and chocolate.

Then, with everything – putting up the tent, eating, writing, brushing teeth – done, came the pre-sleep time to think, the time to create monsters, to raise the spirit of the bogeyman. The mist did not help. The cloak was oppressive, as if the world was silently closing in about me. Arran was just seven miles away across the still waters of the Sound of Bute, but remained invisible. Think about something positive: women, chocolate biscuits, winning the Isle of Jura fell race, I urged myself. Out to sea, I heard the hum of a ship's engine motoring across the bay, seemingly approaching my beach, its lights focused on my tent. I imagined the crew was searching for me, reporting my position to the farmer, who would soon be paying me an angry visit, armed with a shotgun and a couple of snarling dogs. They were ridiculous thoughts.

I zipped up the outer sheet and assumed the defenceless position, trying to shut out the big, bad outside world. Every noise – the tweet of a bird, the lapping of the waves, the wind rustling the grass – pointed to an unknown danger, pointed to something truly awful. I thought about my inner peace, and then the axeman, the dreaded axeman. Not the axeman, anything but the axeman, I beseeched my weary brain. Damn these voices in my head, these thoughts.

It took me a long while to get to sleep. If only my reflections on inner peace and the axeman had come to mind in a different order.

4

Colonsay

From the lone shieling of the misty island
Mountains divide us, and the waste of seas-
Yet still the blood is strong, the heart is Highland,
And we in dreams behold the Hebrides.

Canadian Boat Song

❧

Oban Bay was sparkling, dazzling in late-afternoon sunshine. The sky was picture postcard blue and cloudless. The
sea gleamed turquoise, with the breeze ruffling the surface
into rows of miniature white horses.

I was bound for the Hebrides, a vast archipelago of
Gaelic-speaking, sparsely-populated lands adorning the
north-west coast of mainland Scotland. The name given
to these fragments of land derives from the Norse word
Havbredey, meaning the isles at the edge of the sea. The
literal implication of these words is that the Hebrides lie on
the lip of a flat Earth, with the world ending in an enormous
waterfall plunging into unknown depths. The Hebrides are
spectacular – but not that spectacular.

Edge can mean whatever one desires, be it cultural,
economic, emotional, geographic, philosophical or politi-
cal. The Hebrides are complicated; they have many edges.
The isles can be bleak (but never ugly), a wind can blow for
days and winters are long and stormy. Yet there is a beauty
here unparalleled on our sceptred isle – an ever-changing

vision of beach, loch, machair, moor and mountain beneath the widest of skies.

MV *Lord of the Isles* nudged along the Sound of Kerrera, the bulk of Mull appearing to the west as the ship entered the bigger, darker waters of the Firth of Lorn. Setting a course for the dropping sun, the vessel stayed close to the shore of Seil, an island wedded to the mainland by a single-arched bridge built in the 18th century, grandly named the Bridge over the Atlantic. Beyond Seil were the white-washed cottages of unattached Easdale, one of the Slate Islands and the host of the annual world skimming stone championships.

A clutch of islands now filled the eastern and southern horizons: Luing, which one day may be linked to the mainland via Seil if a causeway is built between the two islands, the Garvellachs, Lunga and Eilean Dubh Mor, with Cruach Scarba, the 449-metre zenith of Scarba, looming above them all. And then, the greatest sight of our two-and-a-quarter-hour voyage: the Paps of Jura, three conical mountains soaring almost to 800 metres, each crowned by a tuft of grey cloud, like a trio of top hats.

Colonsay – bare, low-lying and silhouetted to the west – could not compete with the grandeur of Jura. Yet as we approached the island's ferry terminal at Scalasaig, I tingled with excitement at the prospect of venturing onto this wild and – for me – unexplored island.

I walked along a single-track road, away from the terminal, away from Scalasaig, moving onto a verge to allow the occasional car to sweep past, until I reached The Colonsay, a white-washed hotel overlooking the village. Leaving the road, I followed a track cross-country, climbing towards a telecommunications mast erected on a knoll above Scalasaig. Upon reaching the highest point of the path, I threw off my rucksack and drank so hastily from a bottle of water I choked on the contents. Temporarily abandoning my belongings, I left the main thoroughfare and proceeded along a narrow, winding route across gorse-covered slopes, leading to the 136-metre summit of Beinn nan Gudairean. The loftiest point on the island – Carn an Eoin – was only seven metres higher. A weather-beaten toposcope erected in 1938 marked the top of Beinn nan Gudairean. From here, I glimpsed the rocky west coast of Colonsay for the first time and I fancied the faraway land I could see to the south – just visible in the haze – was Ireland.

Beinn nan Gudairean is a MacPhie, Colonsay's answer to the Munros. While the Munros are the 283 Scottish mountains of 3000ft (914 metres) or higher, the MacPhies are mere molehills, defined as the 21 'eminences' on Colonsay where the land punctures the 300ft (91-metre) contour. It is possible to visit all of the MacPhies in a 20-mile excursion. The 22nd MacPhie, Beinn Oronsay, is on neighbouring Oronsay, an island linked to Colonsay by a tidal causeway. The MacPhies take their name from the Macfies or the MacDuffies, the medieval chiefs of Colonsay who acted as keepers of the records for the Lords of the Isles. Colonsay and Oronsay remain the ancestral home of Clan Macfie. The island was subsequently passed between the MacDonalds, the Campbells of Argyll and the MacNeils, before it was purchased by Lord Strathcona in 1905. Colonsay continues in the ownership of the Strathcona family, now under the guise of the Colonsay Estate.

Shortly after rejoining the road, I stopped to talk to the first person I had seen since leaving the terminal.

'Just going to the top and back,' the man said, pointing vaguely into the distance. I continued to Kiloran, resisting the temptation of a bunk bed at an estate-run backpacker's lodge.

Kiloran Bay is an arresting, mile-long stretch of golden sand, backed by dunes and hemmed in by rocks. It is Colonsay's flagship beach – a giant picture of Kiloran decorated the wall of the Cal Mac waiting room in Oban and the bay was pictured on the front cover of the current Ordnance Survey map for Jura and Colonsay. Kiloran is the type of magical beach a child might draw, conjured from an imagination non-cynical enough to believe in perfection.

With daylight fading, my attention switched from whimsical musings to practicalities, principally finding somewhere to camp. I scouted around for some time, seeking a place to pitch my tent that would be sheltered from an increasingly brisk wind blowing off the Atlantic. I eventually chose a spot on a raised grassy bank above the beach. I cooked pasta with the tent door shut to prevent the wind blowing out the gas flame, but I threw open the flap again to eat and watch the sunset over the bay. The western sky was ablaze, a mesmerising pink and red. Hurriedly finishing my meal, I raced towards the sea to be as close as possible when the sun finally slipped beneath the horizon. Slowly but surely, the ball of burning yellow vanished, leaving only the moon to light the Hebridean sky.

I surrounded the tent with a ring of rocks hauled from a stream that cut a channel across the beach. Sitting inside listening to the wind clawing at the canvas, I was unwilling to undress until I was convinced the tent would not be blown away in the night. The wind always sounds worse inside than out, I reminded myself. A stiff breeze outside can sound like a hurricane on the other side of the canvas.

But, ominously, the wind was strengthening. I bowed to the inevitable. Staying put would mean no sleep. The sound of the ceaselessly rippling tent and the nagging doubt that the precious structure could be damaged or – the worst case scenario – ripped from the ground with me inside, would see to that.

Off I went in the near darkness, scampering over the dunes, searching for a new home, one that would afford a great deal more shelter than my beach-side pad. It was now late; I could not afford to be choosy. I found a site some 200 metres back from the beach at the edge of the dunes. It was sheltered from the wind, but close to a farm track and surrounded by dung. It would have to do.

I slept badly: too hot, then too cold, always too uncomfortable. I had pitched the tent on a slope, meaning I was forever rolling to the lower side. At about 2am I had turned around, putting my feet where my head had been, which seemed to help, and I eventually found sleep. I woke at 9am, bad-tempered and groggy, as if hungover, and crawled out to inspect my crude camping site. The tent was half-pitched over ferns and stinging nettles, while the natural shelter this spot afforded meant it was also favoured by cows and sheep, hence the proliferation of dung.

I was once asked what a wild camp smells of. I am sure I uttered some romantic nonsense by way of an answer: fragrant heather, frying bacon, morning dew. Now I know what I should have said.

I returned to the beach, using my rucksack as a windbreak while I cooked porridge on the sand. My mood gradually softened: I could think of few finer places to eat breakfast. I concealed my bag in a deep dune and set off to explore the north of Colonsay. The rucksack contained all my worldly possessions, everything I needed to survive – tent, sleeping bag, roll mat, cooking equipment, food, books, maps, clothes and shoes – but I had no qualms about leaving it, for many hours if necessary, even somewhere far more exposed.

Colonsay, like many of its Hebridean neighbours, is virtually crime-free. The rarity of law-breaking in such places was demonstrated in 2006 when the trifling misdemeanour – by the standards of any British town or city – of stealing cash from a home in Colonsay made national headlines. The crime was the first of its kind ever recorded on the island. A visiting contractor from Glasgow was working on a project to improve disabled access to the island's primary school when he sneaked into the house of a pensioner, taking £60 from a money box. He was unable to make a quick escape as the next ferry to the mainland was not due to leave the island for two days. Islanders in Scalasaig quickly grew suspicious of the man's behaviour and alerted Colonsay's only police officer. With no cells on Colonsay, islanders kept watch over the man until the ferry arrived. He admitted his guilt and was ordered to pay £400 – more than six times what he stole – by a sheriff at Oban Sheriff Court. The *Herald* reported at the time that not only was the offence the first recorded theft from a home on Colonsay, it was also the first crime of any sort on the island since a series of car thefts in 2004.

The transgression rocked a trusting community proud to keep their front doors unlocked, sparking, according to the media, a 'rare anxiety' among residents. But islanders vowed they would not start bolting their doors.

'We'll carry on as before on the island. We have a great faith in human nature, which remains. It's not as if you can get a smash and grab or anything here. There are only three boats a week, so that's not exactly a quick getaway,' a defiant islander was quoted as saying in the *London Evening Standard*.

I walked north, first along the entire, empty tract of Kiloran Bay, then following a rough track past raised beaches and a farm, to reach Balnahard Bay. It was impossibly gorgeous, surpassing even Kiloran Bay. Here the sand was white, the colour of the water a Caribbean hue. The outlook extended to all the islands I had glimpsed on the ferry the previous day: the Garvellachs, Jura, Mull and Scarba the most prominent. The Paps had removed their top hats.

The peace was shattered. A group of students poured over the machair, jumping off the dunes and onto the beach. They whooped with delight. I heard one of the girls call out breathlessly: 'This is amazing.' Clothes were wrenched off revealing pink skin, towels were laid out, sun tan lotion applied. Two more students followed, both carrying sea kayaks, then a third riding a quad bike. The driver steered the vehicle across the tide line, throwing up a shower of water behind, and performed an elaborate figure of eight before parking by his friends. For all its loveliness, Balnahard had been perfect because it was mine, mine alone, as if I had discovered it and been the first person to leave footprints on virgin sand. The cockle strand had now lost its virginity; it was marked by the wheels of a quad bike.

I walked the six road miles to Scalasaig in an unhurried, dreamlike state. It was one of those rare moments in life when I had nowhere to go, no-one to see and nothing I had to do. It was exhilarating, but terrifying. My existence for the moment lacked any purpose. Maybe this is the beginning of finding my inner peace, I thought? The world seemed even brighter, even purer, than yesterday. The sun beamed from a cloudless sky, although a bitter north wind continued to blow.

The shop in Scalasaig – the only one on the island – was closed when I arrived in the village. I had read that the store sold a surprisingly diverse range of goods, from egg plants and 'exotic muesli' to the 'ingredients for hummus' and Inverawe smoked salmon. But however well-stocked, a shop that is shut until tomorrow was not much use to me today, particularly as my food supplies had almost expired. Fortunately, there was also a café, The Pantry, in Scalasaig.

I am not a good customer at such establishments. I order the cheapest dish on the menu, ask for tap water rather than paying for a drink and typically overstay my welcome by reading or writing long after my plate has been cleared.

Colonsay's link to the outside world is ferry traffic, hence a little community has grown up around the pier and terminal at Scalasaig. Arrivals were first greeted by an A-board saying: 'Welcome to Colonsay – the smallest island in the world with its own brewery.' Opened in 2007, Colonsay Brewery produces ales, beers and lagers, using the brewing methods of the monks who once ruled Colonsay and Oronsay as inspiration.

Three roads break off from the terminal. One passes a wooden coastguard hut, before reaching the dead-end of The Pantry. A second climbs west, running alongside The Colonsay and onto Kilchattan, the island's other main area of settlement. The third, which passes the general store and a post office, a line of homes at Glas Aird, and twists and turns to Kiloran, was the route I had walked earlier. Opposite the shop was a single petrol pump, where the price of unleaded was an eye-watering £1.48 per litre. Still, the residents of Colonsay could not complain. The *Oban Times* had reported earlier in the week that the price of unleaded at the community-owned petrol station on Coll had spiralled to £1.53 per litre.

Talking of newspapers, should islanders or tourists want a Tuesday or Wednesday edition, they have to wait until Thursday. Or if they want a Saturday or Sunday newspaper, the earliest they will see one is Monday. Such are the complications and quirks of island life. A war memorial in the village commemorates the 19 men who fell in World War I and II. Of the 19 names, six were MacNeils.

And that is Scalasaig.

Even as I walked away from the village, I knew I did not have enough food. I would survive on porridge and instant mashed potato, I reasoned. I walked southwards, a long, lonely trudge on road, stopping at a picnic area overlooking The Strand, a mile-and-a-half broad expanse of mud, sand and water, separating Colonsay and Oronsay. I camped on a bumpy grass shelf above the shoreline, hiding my tent behind a rocky knoll, giving protection from the breeze.

Later I was descending heathery Beinn Eibhne, another MacPhie, when I saw two head-bowed figures slowly pushing mountain bikes across The Strand. I walked out to meet them.

'We've been stranded for 12 hours,' the main said. He walked in sopping wet socks, carrying a sodden pair of shoes under an arm.

'We were cut off by the tide,' the woman, bedraggled and sunburned, explained.

I told them of my plan to run across the causeway to Oronsay tomorrow.

The man pulled a face. 'Good luck,' he said. 'You'll have three hours – one-and-a-half hours before low tide and the same after. Leave it any later and you'll end up like us.'

I watched patiently, waiting for the glistening sea in The Strand to retreat, revealing an underlay of grey, smelly sand. Deeming the sea was far enough out, I set off, running steadily with a keen wind at my back, following the marks of car tyres that the sea had failed to wash away. The sand was dark and sludgy, a contrast to the white grains sprinkled across the beaches of Balnahard and Kiloran,

44

making the going hard. As I neared Oronsay's north coast, the tide was still receding, with a narrow channel of water still between the island and I. A group of walkers stood on the edge of the channel, prevaricating about the tides, not wanting to get their feet wet. I ran between them, splashing through calf-deep water to gain land.

The most significant visitor to set foot on Oronsay is believed to have been St Columba, the 6th century Irish prince who travelled to Scotland with a mission to convert the Picts to Christianity. On the way to Iona, where St Columba established a monastery in 563, transforming the island into a renowned centre of Christian learning, he is thought to have landed on Oronsay. It was, however, St Oran who gave his name to the island after he founded a monastery here, also in 563. St Columba may have ruled out the possibility of creating his own monastery on Oronsay because the island was in sight of the Irish coast. An Augustinian priory was built on the site of St Oran's original monastery in the 14th century and the ruins of the buildings, including a four-metre high Celtic cross erected on a mound, remain in place today.

I had intended to climb Beinn Oronsay, but access to the hill was forbidden by the RSPB due to the presence of nesting birds. I made directly for the priory instead, with the advantage of running over walking giving me a head start on any other visitors, enabling me to explore the ruins in undisturbed solitude. I ran south from the priory, leaving a turf track for a short while to trot along a windswept beach, a cerulean sea lapping its shore. Continuing my progress, I passed a grass landing strip, the grazing sheep parting as I approached and geese honking overhead.

The Paps of Jura were always there, always to the east, rising peerlessly. Each time I gazed at them, they appeared bolder and more striking. They made me shudder too, for in four days I would be running up and down their scree-smothered sides. A trot around Oronsay would not prepare me for that. At Rubha Caol, the southern tip of the island, I turned to face the frantic gusts, following faint corridors of trodden grass created by the hooves of cattle and sheep, stretching along the line of the east coast. A path leading to an isolated cottage overlooking two beaches led me back to the priory track. It was now low tide on The Strand, with at least 20 travellers – cyclists, walkers and some in cars – making the pilgrimage to Oronsay. Among them were the students I had seen at Balnahard Bay.

I sloshed through puddles of warm sea water to regain Colonsay, sinking wearily to the ground next to my tent. I read until I could no longer keep my eyes open and I dozed in the sun. Unwilling to force down a further helping of porridge, I cooked the remainder of the mashed potato using the last of my water. I was dizzy, afflicted by hunger and tiredness, as I retraced my steps back to Scalasaig. I would have attempted to thumb a lift, but there was no traffic. It was a relief to see the pier again, for it meant food. The shop would be open today.

After eating and regaining some strength, I clambered uphill to the monument overlooking the village, a memorial to Lord Colonsay, given by the people of the island. I looked across Colonsay lovingly, delighting in the view. This was a place so remote. I wondered if I would stand here again, if I would see Colonsay again. Perhaps it was best if I do not. For in my mind, Colonsay will always be a place of faultlessness, of endless blue skies, of flawless white beaches, a land of glorious contemplation, freedom and seclusion. It could never be as perfect again.

5

Islay

Always carry a large flagon of whisky in case of snakebite
and furthermore always carry a small snake.

W.C. *Fields*

❧

Whisky was the blether of the bar in the Port Askaig Hotel,
the first watering hole arriving travellers from Colonsay or
Jura fall into. Islay – the Queen of the Hebrides – was
midway through Fèis Ìle, the island's annual celebration of
malt and music. 'The isle with a song in its heart and music
in its soul,' the festival programme sentimentalised.

Islay has eight active whisky distilleries, some with his-
tories dating back more than two centuries, the newest aged
only five. The opening of a ninth distillery, Port Charlotte,
was imminent. All bar one of the island's distilleries touch
the coast, with their evocative, globally-recognised brand
names daubed in gigantic black script on white back-
grounds facing out to sea.

The distilleries would take it in turns to stage open events
during Fèis Ìle, with hundreds of whisky tourists touring the
plants and, most importantly, sampling the wares. Tomorrow it was the opportunity of the young and the old:
Kilchoman, Islay's junior distillery and the first to be built
on the island for 124 years, and Isle of Jura, which was
marking its 200th anniversary. Kilchoman promised a tour
led by the distillery manager, a tasting session in its ware-
house, an 'exclusive' single cask bottling, folk music and a

47

seafood barbecue. Craighouse-based Isle of Jura, admitted to Fèis Ìle by virtue of its proximity to Islay, had a similar offering, with admission also including a 'distillery gift' and free travel on the Port Askaig-Feolin ferry.

'It's the water, you see. That's what makes Islay whisky the best whisky in the world.'

'The water? Really?' I shrugged. I had rashly enquired about the significance of Islay whisky. Was it better than a Speyside whisky, for instance? Or an Easter Ross whisky? It was an ignorant question. An ignorant question to pose in a bar overflowing with whisky connoisseurs, like asking a Celtic supporter what Jock Stein ever won.

The man tried to explain again. He was English and clutched a glass of whisky – presumably one of the Islay brands – in his right hand. His cheeks and nose glowed; his red, rolling eyes gave away his inebriation. The bar had fallen silent. I could sense all ears were now listening to our conversation.

'It is the quality of the water that makes Islay whisky what it is. It's unique,' he repeated. An elderly fellow on a neighbouring table nodded in agreement, raising his glass.

I was sceptical. 'But isn't the water the same water that falls on the Highlands, or Skye, or anywhere else in Scotland?'

It was his turn to shrug. He had no explanation. 'Uisge beatha,' he whispered in imprecise Gaelic. 'Water of life.'

The weather had turned: rain, and a northerly wind, ice-cold for late-May. The conditions altered my mood. I had camped in the dry, on a strip of flat grass overlooking the lifeboat station on the Sound of Islay. Now the tent was drenched. The canvas would need to dry out before I could sleep in it again. Camping was my only option, however heavy the rain. Islay was brimful of tourists, with every room in bed and breakfasts and hotels snapped up, and every hostel bed accounted for.

I caught a bus, mulling over a loose plan to travel as far as Bowmore, Islay's administrative centre, before going to Port Charlotte later in the day. On the way, I wanted to stop at Finlaggan, the ancient powerbase of the Lords of the Isles, from where successive rulers presided over a Hebridean empire for hundreds of years. The chance passed me by; I did not get off the bus. Nor did I disembark at Bowmore, rattling across a rain-soaked peatscape to Port Ellen instead.

Port Ellen was miserable: damp, grey and windswept. I mithered about what to do, irritated at my hesitancy. I moped and sulked, deliberated and wavered, then, at last, I came to a firm decision. When on Islay, drink whisky. I would go to a distillery. After all, it was Fèis Île. But which one? I was too late for the tour at Kilchoman, while Isle of Jura was too far away. The three distilleries east of Port Ellen – Ardbeg, Lagavulin and Laphroaig – were my best options. I started to walk along the road to the first one, Laphroaig, but turned back when it started to rain heavily again. I retreated to Port Ellen, where I boarded a bus to Ardbeg.

Arriving at drizzly Ardbeg, a small, white-washed distillery on the rim of a rocky Islay cove, it was hard to imagine I was entering a realm of sublime, unsurpassed greatness.

'The ultimate single Islay malt Scotch whisky,' the strapline of Ardbeg proudly boasts. The swank is with good reason. Ardbeg is not only the finest whisky on Islay; it is the finest whisky on the planet.

Ardbeg whiskies were twice heralded as the best on Earth in the late 2000s. The distillery's Ten-year-old expression was named world whisky of the year and Scotch single malt of the year in 2008 by *Jim Murray's Whisky Bible*, with identical accolades going to its Uigeadail expression a year later. The Ardbeg dominance was broken in 2010; its Supernova expression was a runner-up in the world whisky of the year category, although distillers were consoled when the whisky was adjudged the top Scotch for the third consecutive year. Murray himself has described Ardbeg as 'unquestionably the greatest distillery to be found on Earth'.

I put my name down for a distillery tour, and with an hour to fill before its commencement, I went in search of Shortie, Ardbeg's Jack Russell mascot. I tried the Old Kiln café first – surely a favourite haunt of a titbit-hunting dog – before taking my canine pursuit outside. Shortie was nowhere to be seen. Perhaps it was his day off?

I looked to the shop to distract me, perusing the visitor's book. The gushing comments and names of British visitors were outstripped by tourists from Austria, Germany, Israel, Spain, Sweden and the US. The shop reminded me of a football club store, awash with branded merchandise. The numerous garments – beanie hats, berets, body warmers, cycling jerseys, jumpers, scarves, sweatshirts, ties, waterproof jackets – were adorned or embossed with the Ardbeg logo. And – because only an alcoholic can get away with drinking whisky directly from the bottle – there were tasting glasses, tumblers of various sizes and water jugs. The true whisky fanatic would, I am sure, also purchase a tin of peat cones – basically, lumps of peat that can be set alight – to heighten the whisky-drinking experience. There was even a dog collar featuring the Ardbeg knotwork and a Shortie motif.

'No self-respecting canine should be seen without this stylish leather dog collar,' advised the marketing blurb.

Shortie will be bringing out his own expression next.

Put the name of Ardbeg on something, anything, it seemed, and it will sell. And the Americans or Swedes who had travelled thousands of miles across seas to visit this Hebridean outpost were prepared to spend. I watched an American woman deliberating over a £65 waterproof jacket. I wanted to shake her, tell her not to waste her money. The woman undoubtedly had money to waste. She bought the jacket; it would be a talking point once she returned home.

Founded in 1815, decades of whisky-distilling at Ardbeg ended in 1981 when the plant was mothballed. The boom years of the 1970s were followed by a plunge in global sales. The site's owner, Allied Distillers, which also ran Laphroaig, chose to concentrate its efforts on the neighbouring distillery, before reopening Ardbeg for small-scale production in 1989. It was not the start of a new dawn; in 1996 Ardbeg was closed again. The distillery was sold to Glenmorangie the following year – a move that led to a transformation in the fortunes of Ardbeg. Full production resumed in 1998. Then in 2004, Glenmorangie was acquired by Moet Hennessy – Louis Vuitton, giving Ardbeg a major corporate backer. Success in awards was mirrored by production; the distillery churned out more than one million litres of whisky in 2009.

The tour was what one might expect from a visit to a whisky distillery, a walk through the four main stages of production – milling, mashing, fermenting and distilling. As I am on the subject of whisky, it would perhaps be useful to explain the whisky-making process. Unfortunately, I switched off during the tour; I simply did not listen. Early on, I recall the guide saying something about barley being mixed with water. Thereafter, I nodded and smiled at seemingly appropriate moments and when we made eye contact. I am sure her speech was interesting, riveting even –

but I chose not to hear. The smell, however, was lovely – comforting, intoxicating and warm.

Once whisky's raw materials have been milled, mashed, fermented and distilled, the liquid is put in casks and locked away, for at least three years by law, but more likely 10. The whisky we had seen in production would not be tasted by the public until at least 2020.

There were four Germans among our tour party, with one of their rank taking it upon himself to ask *the* water question, saving me the potential embarrassment. Now I was listening. The guide shook her head incredulously. 'It is rainwater,' she said, flatly, 'falling on the same hills, draining into the same burns, which is then used by Ardbeg, Lagavulin and Laphroaig as a water source.' The earth Islay's water flows through gives its whiskies their peaty, smoky distinction, she continued, but the notion that the water has some kind of magical power is nonsense. I sensed she had been asked this question once too often.

Back at the shop, I introduced myself to the Germans. The 'whisky brothers', as they called themselves, said they planned to visit each of Islay's distilleries during Fèis Ìle. They were here only for whisky. For them, the week-long visit was a pilgrimage, a thrilling journey to learn where the whisky they drank around the fire in their houses or in bars in their home town of Aachen was created. Later that day, they would climb into the hills above the distillery to taste and touch the water in the burns that are used as the source of Ardbeg's manufacturing process. That is devotion.

Stefan's love affair with whisky had taken time to spark. The physician visited Scotland in a motorcycling tour in 2002, stopping off at the Glenlivet distillery in Speyside to sample the whisky. As the liquid touched the back of his throat, he gagged – a typical first reaction to whisky. The journey later took him to Skye and the Talisker distillery.

He drank again, not gagging this time, and began to appreciate and understand the geographic identities and tastes of Scotland's whiskies.

He returned to the islands in 2007, this time to test the whiskies of Orkney. 'I could begin to taste the difference,' he smiled. 'I knew I loved it. But I didn't come home and say, 'I need a whisky,' because you don't need a lot to enjoy it.'

'What about American whisky, Irish whisky . . .?'

Stefan cut me off. 'Scottish, always Scottish. I don't like Bourbon or Irish. Scotland's have so much more flavour, more love inside. Caol Ila, for example – you drink it in the evening and you can still taste it in the morning.'

Volker, another physician, joined us, clutching a newly-bought, Ardbeg-branded cagoule. I bit my lip. 'Tell this man about whisky,' Stefan said, pointing in my direction. Volker was a whisky romantic. He had been the one to ask the question about the water; no doubt he wanted his fancy of magic raindrops falling on Islay to be true.

'When I drink whisky, I taste the place it has come from, the landscape, the water, the people who made it, the spirit of the area.'

The spirit of the area – Volker's phrase captured me.

I understood. I had sniggered at what I thought were ridiculous anecdotes of whisky-enthusiasts shedding tears as they glimpsed Islay for the first time. But now I understood. Sipping Ardbeg, Caol Ila or Laphroaig in Germany, Sweden or the US would awaken the sense of Islay – a land of wide skies, fast-flowing burns, peaty hills, rocky shorelines and sandy beaches – in the mind of a whisky-drinker. To be here, to stand on Islay, to drink the drink in its birthplace, must multiply the pleasure many times over.

The guide plonked a bottle on a table before us, unscrewed the top and poured generously, thrusting a glass into each of our eager hands. Oh, how our eyes lit up. A chance to drink the distillery's present crown jewel: a 2010 Supernova, billed by Ardbeg as 'a deeper, earthier character with the same phenomenal peatiness as the 2009 edition'. Whatever that meant. The stuff does not come cheap, costing about £80 per bottle.

I was about to gulp when I saw the others sniffing and swilling, breathing in the aroma. They closed their eyes in apparent ecstasy. I copied, giving the liquid a deep, deliberate sniff, slopping it around my glass. The Germans babbled enthusiastically in their own language. Almost 20 seconds went by and still no-one had tasted. I took the plunge, putting the glass to my lips and swallowing. It was strong, very peaty. I coughed, trying not to pull a face. I did not like it, not at all. The Supernova was overpowering for a palette unused to whisky, let alone Islay whisky. I tasted again. It was marginally better.

'Lovely,' I said. I was not going to admit to not liking something that cost £80. Yet the whisky was wasted on me. I did not appreciate, did not realise, what I was drinking.

Fortunately, there are others who do. This is how the US whisky expert John Hansell described the 2010 expression: 'Here's what I'm picking up, in somewhat descending order in taste profile: leafy smoke, coal tar, mocha fudge with dark chocolate chips, smoked olive, peppered seaweed salad, fruit (lemon, lime), genever, brine-tinged grass, and (with some coaxing) floral notes (violet?).' There speaks a man with an astonishing nose for whisky. Although it made me laugh aloud the first time I read it – mocha fudge with dark chocolate chips? Had we drunk the same drink?

Volker finished his dram and helped himself to another while the guide's back was turned. The whisky brothers looked contented. An elderly man in our group had reddened slightly. A young couple clinked glasses, exchanging flirty smiles. I felt a dizzying warmth trickle through my veins, ripple across my forehead. I poured myself another dram. The whisky tasted better with every sip. So what if I could not detect peppered seaweed salad and brine-tinged grass. Slaintè.

Tipsily, I made my way to Port Charlotte, changing buses at Bowmore. The glow of alcohol wore off quickly; the mundane reality of having to find somewhere to camp took hold. The vacillation of the morning returned, as I fretted about where to lay my head. There was no shortage of options. That was the problem. Free camping was permitted in a park opposite the White Hart hotel in Port Ellen, while an assistant at the tourist centre in Bowmore suggested camping wild on a beach south-west of the town. Neither prospect appealed. After lonely nights on Bute and Colonsay, I craved the company of others, even if that company was unspeaking and in another tent. I simply wanted to be around fellow humans.

On the edge of Port Charlotte, I found Port Mòr, a community-run caravan and camping site, its facilities powered by a ground-source heating system, solar panels and a wind turbine, its ground level, dung and rock-free. With a strong wind blowing, my once-sodden tent was dry in minutes. I showered for the first time since leaving Oban, staying in the cubicle for a long while. Such moments had become rare luxuries.

I ran for the last time before I would cross swords with Jura in two days, the exertion rather nullifying the effect of showering. My athletic efforts over the previous months had been sporadic, inevitably disrupted by my island journey. I have not done enough, anything like enough, I told myself, as I laced my trainers. Knocking back drams of whisky at lunchtime would not help my cause either. Jura was 10 miles shorter than a marathon, but would take at least an hour longer than a 26.2-mile race would. Yet it was not the distance or the time that had me unduly worried – it was those terrifying Paps.

It was dusk, my favourite time to run, when I strode away from Port Charlotte, clapping my hands together to keep warm. I followed the road south, before clambering over a fence and climbing a slope churned up by the hooves of cows to a cairn overlooking Loch Indaal. My stride was long and relaxed, my breathing light; it was the strongest I had felt in weeks. I paused by the cairn. An almost full moon shone across the silent water of Loch Indaal. Belief surged through me. Jura might not be so bad, I speculated, the Paps might be merciful. I hoped.

6

Jura

Last night I was with you in my dreams
across in Jura of the Cold Bens . . .
Traditional 18th century Jura song

Jura was grimacing. Across the churning waters of the Sound of Islay, the island glowered imperiously, a vision of grand terror. The beautiful, brutal Paps were wreathed in cloud. Shifting shadows flashed ominously about the island. Frothy waves thrashed sand and shingle margins. Apart from a clutch of buildings at Feolin and a pier reaching out into a choppy sea, Jura appeared void of civilisation, a bleak, untouched land.

There has been an annual hill race on Jura since 1983. Starting and finishing at Craighouse, the axis of island life, the wild chase is over 16 miles of relentlessly rough and pathless terrain. Competitors must cross seven mountain summits, three of them the Paps. The fastest runners take three-and-half hours; the slowest closer to seven. The race's total ascent – 2300 metres – is akin to stacking Scafell Pike on top of Ben Nevis, starting from sea level, and climbing them both. Details of conditions and routes provided by the organisers go something like this: 'Ascent on steep scree slope for 600 metres;' 'steep descent on rock and grass;' 'steep ascent by gully or ridge;' 'direct descent to lochans impossible due to sheer precipice on north side of Beinn Shiantaidh;' 'boggy and rough going.' One word crops up repeatedly: steep.

Participants are given the freedom to follow a course of their own choosing, enabling an experienced individual to exploit his or her local knowledge of the optimum running ground. But there is a proviso. Competitors must visit eight checkpoints – each of the seven summits and a final one at Three Arch Bridge, a Thomas Telford creation hewn in 1804, marking the start of a three-mile road section to the finish. For the mountain runner, whose studded boots are ill-equipped for the hard surface of a road, this concluding section is torture on top of torture. There is no excuse for missing a checkpoint. The result is disqualification.

The race is a serious, many would say ludicrous, under-taking, demanding endurance, stamina and – in poor weather – first-rate navigation skills, making it an occasion for the masochist. Overflowing quantities of bloody-mind-edness are *de rigueur*. Even then, runners must prove they have the mettle to be welcomed onto the Jura start line. Entrants are required to have finished two – to use hill running jargon – AL-standard races, meaning their Jura qualifiers should feature more than 75 metres of vertical ascent per mile and be at least 12 miles in length. There are few of these about. Even the flagship race in the Scottish hill running calendar, Ben Nevis, is considered too soft to meet the robust entry requirements of Jura. Despite the ascent, the distance, the terrain, the difficulty in attaining a place and even the logistics of getting to Jura, the race is perpe-tually oversubscribed.

There were three of us, all runners, on a bus to Craig-house, an eight-mile drive from Feolin on Jura's only public road. The two others were from Middlesbrough and had taken part in the Fellsman – a 62-mile yomp across the Yorkshire Dales – three weeks earlier, with the younger man having completed the course in a brisk 12 hours. We were dropped off outside the Isle of Jura distillery in the village, where the race would start the following morning.

Dozens of runners had already arrived, pitching tents in a shore side field overlooked by the Jura Hotel, the island's sole hostelry. The competitors typically double Jura's permanent population of 200 for the weekend. Many stay beyond race day, visiting Barnhill, where George Orwell wrote Nineteen Eighty-Four, or travelling north along the Long Road to glimpse the boiling waters of the Corryvreckan whirlpool in the Sound of Jura.

Craighouse was decorated with brown, red and yellow bunting. A race banner hailing the event's 30th anniversary was stretched across a fence. The weather was putting on its finest four-seasons-in-one-day performance, with brilliant sunshine superseded by a cloudburst. A cool breeze continued to blow from the north. But when the sun shone, it was idyllic: campers lying out on the grass, runners recalling previous years' races, sweeping views across the Small Isles of Jura and the Argyll mainland. The backdrop of it all was the heady aroma of whisky fumes emanating from the distillery.

As the afternoon wore on, Craighouse became a hive of activity as people continued to arrive on ferries from the mainland and Islay. Others came by bicycle, two more by kayak. Soon the field was a kaleidoscope of multi-coloured canvas, from my tiny one-man contraption to towering teepees. Runners queued for freshly-arrived bread and milk in the village store. Tea, coffee, sandwiches and an array of cakes were being rapidly consumed in the cooperage next to the distillery. There was a hum of expectation in the air. Some went on a last run, perhaps along the coast road or up the initial slopes of the first hill.

By 9pm it seemed as if everyone had arrived. The tents were tightly packed, at least 60 in all. The sun had gone, but the wind had dropped, bringing out the midges. A neighbouring camper handed me a lukewarm mug of coffee, which was decorated by numerous black bodies floating on the surface within seconds. Refuge had to be sought, either at the pub or inside my tent. I dived under-cover, distracting myself with the race instructions and a map.

The first three checkpoints were on minor hills: Dubh Bheinn, Glas Bheinn and Aonach-bheinn – known affectionately as the Pips – ranging from 499 to 562 metres in altitude. A round of these summits would make a challenging hill race in itself, but in this contest, the Pips are a mere warm-up act to the main event: the Paps. First up would be Beinn a' Chaolais, the longest single ascent of the race, then Beinn an Oir, the highest point at 785 metres, and then Beinn Shiantaidh, holy mountain. By then I might be in need of holy intervention. But still it is not over. After avoiding the 'sheer precipice', a descent through boulder fields is followed by a climb up yet another hill, Corra Bheinn, the fourth highest on the route. The earlier air of contentment in Craighouse had become an air of nervous-ness, of trepidation, in my tent. I imagined similar con-templations were happening in other tents. I folded away the map, silently wished for clear weather and fell asleep.

Long before the Jura race had even pricked my conscious-ness, the much-published novelist Will Self penned his own estimation of the event in a column that graced the pages of the *Independent*. It did not go down well. Enthusiastic about the Paps ('beautiful, conical mountains, their steep sides gleaming with quartzite scree'), he was less endearing about the runners, whom he called 'bandy-legged goaties' with 'spavinous goatie wives and even little kids clip-clop-ping about the hamlet of Craighouse'. I had to look spa-vinous up in a dictionary. I am still not entirely confident of its meaning, although I am sure it is not to be taken as a compliment.

'Now they've pitched their goatie tents and are thrusting their goatie chins towards the Paps and baaaing together, for tomorrow they're going to run up them,' Self wrote. 'The fastest of them will do it in a little over three hours – and let's face it, to do that you have to be more ungulate than human.'

So far, so funny, I thought. But then he ramped up the satire: 'It's disconcerting having the herd in such close proximity – they get to me, and when morning comes I find I have half a mind to pop downstairs, register for the race, and join them. Only half a mind, because although the day dawns bright and fair, and a banner has been unrolled across the road, and a youthful pipe band is working hard to get out of tune, when I go down among the goaties the feral and slightly faecal stench of them is most off-putting.'

Self was at it again a year later, also writing in the *Independent*, this time after he was approached by a pair of disgruntled runners. 'There's something a little bit intimidating about the goaties; they're so damn fit and wiry, they might – quite inadvertently – poke your eye out with one of those horny hands.'

The comedian Dom Joly took a milder approach when he broached the subject of hill running and its aficionados. Joly, also scribing for the *Independent*, remarked that those who take part in a yearly race up and down Heaval on Barra would 'either be shot for trespassing or sectioned as being a bit "funny in the head"' were they to do such things in the Cotswolds. Which amused me. For are not these the same Cotswolds where people hurl themselves down a ski slope-steep hill in pursuit of a tumbling block of Double Gloucester? The highest injury toll at the annual Cooper's Hill gathering was in 1997 when 33 people were treated for various ailments by paramedics. Then in 2010, cheese-rolling was deemed so dangerous (the organisers could not get insurance) that the event was shelved.

Perhaps it is acceptable to run down a hill – breaking bones on the way – in the Cotswolds? But up? In the north of Scotland? What a crazy idea! Joly jovially continued, nevertheless: 'Up here, however, if you see a hill you run up it. They are a tough bunch and it's exactly this kind of activity that keeps them match-fit and ready to fight off another Viking invasion.'

A single blast of a shotgun sent us on our way. The pounding of two hundred pairs of feet on road drowned out the skirl of pipes. The theatrical idiom 'break a leg' was daubed across a saltire hanging from a house yards from the start line – a light-hearted but all too realistic prospect. There was no sign of Will Self. There was, however, the distinctive odour of apprehension in the air. Perhaps that is what Self had meant? My prayer had not been answered. A gloomy blanket of mist had been thrown over Jura in the night, hiding the Paps. 'It will lift,' we were assured. It did – only hours after the race was over.

I was prepared for the worst. A bum bag – re-christened a beltpack by its manufacturer, presumably to give the un-stylish attire a modicum of coolness – was strapped tightly around my waist. Inside were waterproofs, a hat, gloves, a map, compass, whistle, food (in my case, two chocolate bars and a sugar-rich block of tablet) and an empty water bottle. The kit was compulsory; every runner carried the same items. Scrupulous kit checks preceded the race. And there would be random checks at the end, we were warned. Numbered cards were attached to our bags, which we would hand over to a waiting marshal at each checkpoint.

Runners were soon stretched out, climbing in silence and in single-file across boggy ground to the rocky, mist-shrouded summit of Dubh Beinn. The leaders were already a long way ahead. I had been counselled that navigation between the first three checkpoints was as burdensome as route-finding on the Paps. Sensible runners memorise bearings or at least write them down. Even more sensible runners reconnoitre the course. I had done neither. With clag obscuring the next summit, I adopted the policy that it would be more prudent to get lost as part of a group than on my own. So I stayed close to a trio of other runners, refusing to let them out of my sight.

Together we soon gained Glas Bheinn, where we handed over a second card and joyously swept downhill across a wide ridge towards Aonach-bheinn, the lowest of the seven hill top checkpoints. No-one else was in sight. It was as if we were racing among ourselves and all the others had disappeared into the darkness, never to be seen again. Perhaps we had gone the wrong way? But as we neared the checkpoint, I glanced behind. There was a group of at least a dozen athletes, bearing down on us like a pack of hungry wolves. And while I absent-mindedly blundered to the west, the followers swooped north – the right way – leaving me flailing in their wake.

We only had to descend a short way before we emerged out of the mist. The downhill was 'moderate', according to race literature. Much rougher and tougher was to come. But this was alarming, terrifyingly steep. I watched runners that were behind me moments earlier plunging downwards with reckless abandon, first across heather, then quartzite scree, to reach the foot of the glen, seemingly oblivious to the perilous terrain. I froze, analysing and complicating the descent. Just run. Run, run, run, I told myself, and down I went full of fear, ankles jarring, feet burning, teeth rattling.

There was to be no respite. The first Pap, Beinn a' Chaolais, lay in wait, dark and brooding, its summit lost in the greyness. The ascent was cruel and unforgiving: 600 vertical metres, initially up a gully, then across fields of boulders and the occasional ramp of vegetation. There were no paths, only what hill runners call trods – the often indistinct footmarks of where previous walkers and, to use Self's term, 'goaties', have been. It was endless, extremely steep. No-one was running. We crouched with hands on thighs, hauling aching bodies to the top, never stopping.

Underlying the pain was something stronger, something deeper. It was always there, however awful the going got. It was a grim sense of satisfaction (enjoyment would be the wrong word), allied with the rawness of the terrain and the exhilaration of just being there, being part of something. We all shared it. That is why we run up mountains, why we submit happily and willingly to the ordeal.

I descended with one of the leading women, another Jura novice, whom I watched as she appeared to surf down vast shoots of scree. She fell, I fell, and she fell again. Falling is certain. Adrenaline numbs the pain. Rocks ricocheted off my ankles, making me wince. As we began the ascent of Beinn an Oir, she told me to go ahead if she was too slow for me. I tried, but the woman's sure stride took her away from me.

The summit ridge was a fearful place: bleak, misty and wind-blasted, with sharp, unknown drops looming right and left. Once on the ridge, I glimpsed two runners ahead. I must catch them, I told myself. The need to reach them became incalculable. I did not want to descend alone. One started walking and the other did likewise, meaning I was able to slowly reel them in. We united and descended as a trio. I was lazy. I let them do the critical map and compass work, choosing to trust the judgement of these strangers. I had a paper map only; the wet would have ripped it to shreds. I imagined we were attached with a length of elastic and I could not let that band stretch too far, else it would snap. My fear of being alone was now greater than my fear of these hideous descents, for visibility extended to no more than 50 metres in any direction, becoming less as altitude was gained.

The ascent to Beinn Shiantaidh, the last Pap, was a blur. I cannot recall the terrain; I cannot recall who I ran with. What I do remember vividly is working myself into a nervous frenzy about the downhill section to come. 'Descent of north side is very dangerous – sheer drop a short way below the summit,' the race instructions had explicitly cautioned.

A marshal took my sixth card – 'two more to go,' I said aloud – and I descended for 30 seconds. I passed a runner laid out on the ground. I stopped next to him, three times asking him what was wrong. He stared blankly into space. It was only on the last occasion, when I raised my voice to a shout, that he replied he 'just needed to eat something'. That reminded me. I extricated the tablet from my bag. It had become misshapen and mashed, but I threw the lot into my mouth, barely chewing and swallowing quickly. I left the hungry runner alone again, treading carefully downhill. Suddenly, for the first time in more than three hours of running, I was on my own.

Desperate times, desperate measures. I pulled the map out of my bag. I was right – the moisture in the air soaked the paper, obliterating the contours between Beinn Shiantaidh and Cerra Bheinn. I fought to control a rising sense of panic. I traversed the hill for what seemed like two or three minutes, but was probably less than 20 seconds, before about 10 runners appeared from above. I joined them as they galloped across a confused landscape of large boulders, eventually joining a narrow trod as we lost height. They were a focussed bunch. One wore nothing but a vest on his top half, while their maps remained folded in bags.

I glanced at my watch – three hours and seven minutes, the record finishing time clocked by Mark Rigby in the 1994 race. I was still six miles, two checkpoints and one hilltop away from the end.

One-by-one the group passed me. Not that I minded. Had it have been a road race, I would have cursed every rival, as a way of deflecting my personal frustrations on to them. Why am I not faster, fitter, stronger? I would torment myself. Not on Jura. I silently applauded each runner. They were heroes; brave, determined, stubborn heroes.

The final hill, Corra Bheinn, sometimes generously referred to as Jura's fourth Pap, loomed ahead. I struggled up, at times on all fours, pleading for the top. As a one-time member of Inverness Harriers, my Scottish club mates would taunt me with cries of 'soft southern bastard' if I so much as uttered a comment on the steepness of a slope. Who was the 'soft southern bastard' today? Now to locate the summit. I had listened to horror stories of runners having been disqualified for failing to find the checkpoint in poor weather. I dreaded that prospect. Imagine coming all this way and falling short? Yet I had no such difficulties. Reaching the top, I wondered how they could have been unsuccessful.

I set off downhill, knowing that I no longer had to go up, forgetting that going down can often be just as hard. The run to the road was as endless as the ascent of Beinn a' Chaolais. My energy levels plummeted, morale waned and ankles throbbed. My face was scorched, as if I had spent a day in the sun, not the mist. Scree that had rolled into my right shoe on the descent from Beinn a' Chaolais dug into my foot. The little stones would trickle under my toes, hide beneath the arch or dig into the sole. Sometimes it was agony; sometimes I forget they were there, as they rolled to a place that caused less hurt. For the hundredth time, I told myself to take off the shoe and remove the offending rocks. But that would mean stopping, and I doubted my cold and shaky hands would be able to unravel a double knot.

The ground became increasingly boggy as I neared the Corran River and occasionally a leg would plunge calf-deep into a stinking pit, forcing me to use all my remaining energy to haul the limb free. Ahead a little crowd had gathered on Three Arch Bridge to cheer on the runners. I passed beneath one of the arches and climbed away from the river to meet the road, buoyed by the presence of others.

Three miles to go, three little miles – an insignificant distance, an easy jog on another day. I ate the last of my food. The chocolate had melted next to my skin. The blissful sensation of running on a flat, stable surface was balanced by a burning ache in my ankles, shins and knees, caused by the pounding on the road. I passed two runners within five minutes, but I could see no others ahead. No-one was to catch me. It was calm and peaceful at sea level. Midges fussed about me. I wondered how far I had gone, for the scenery seemed unaltered. The Small Isles did not appear to be moving. I seemed to be running in slow motion. I could have stopped at the roadside and fallen asleep. I imagined these were the last miles I would ever run. Temporarily bluffing my legs seemed to give me the motivation to continue when all I wanted to do was cease movement.

The pier at Craighouse at last appeared, then the chimney of the distillery, and I knew I was very nearly home. Sleep could wait. I looked at my watch repeatedly, as if I was on the cusp of breaking a world record. Finding a final burst of enthusiasm, I sprinted over the humped back bridge in the village, passed the 'break a leg' saltire and crossed the finish line, culminating my Jura race in a shade under four-and-a-half hours, I staggered and stopped. I felt someone pat me on the back. Another runner grasped my hand, mumbling 'good run'.

I was 58th, more than an hour behind the winner, Bingley runner Rob Jebb. For another two hours, runners poured over the finish line, hailing from the hill-running cliques of Britain: Ambleside and Carnethy, to Eryri and Malvern. Numerous awards were given out in a cooperage-staged prize-giving: to the top ten; the leading men and women in their age categories, right up to the over-50s, known as super-veterans; the highest place Jurachs and Ileachs; and to two runners who had completed 21 races.

And then the drinking started. Weary runners rehydrated with beer and whisky. The Jura Hotel was brimful, spirits high. The alcohol flowed. The fastest and the slowest drank together. Anyone arriving at Craighouse that night would have laughed at the notion we were fit and disciplined mountain athletes. The party eventually moved to the village hall for a ceilidh, with music and shrieks from the pier continuing until well into the small hours of the morning.

It was about 3am when I wobbled to my tent, singing quietly to myself. I was drunk and could not sleep. My head was ringing. After an hour, I gave up and packed up. I very slowly walked the eight miles to Feolin, watching dawn break over Islay and Jura, arriving there at 7am. I felt atrocious. The taste in my mouth was vile. The whisky had been a bad idea. The only food I had was a tin of chicken curry. A foul breakfast, I hungrily ate it all the same.

After catching a bus across Islay to the ferry terminal at Port Ellen, a vessel was approaching Kintyre when a big man with a big smile sat opposite me. He was George

Broderick, a Germany-based university professor who devised the Jura course in 1971 and coordinated the first event – then called the Bens of Jura Fell Race – two years later.

Broderick had already established the Manx Mountain Marathon on the Isle of Man when he first visited Jura for the first time in 1970, touring the island in a 1956 vintage Morris Oxford car. It was during a second stay on the island a year later that he conceived the idea of a race over the Paps to 'stretch the competence of the top runners to the limit'. Broderick attempted to set up the race in 1972, with his efforts met by a sceptical reaction from Jurachs. 'One 65-year-old Jura man, a shepherd, said to me in the Jura Hotel bar one evening that he could not understand why people would freely wish to go into the hills,' Broderick said. 'He went up there 'on business' to put his sheep on or take them off the hill. He would never think of going up there otherwise.'

Nevertheless, a skeleton format for the race was established by the autumn of 1972 and three runners offered to reconnoitre the course, reporting that such an exploit was 'feasible'. But Broderick did not want to create 'just another hill race'. He set about establishing an occasion that would enthral and mesmerise runners, captivating them to return year after year. 'It had to be more than a race, as it would need to lock runners into spending a weekend in an out-of-the-way, then little-known, island in the Hebrides. It was a high risk strategy because of Jura's remoteness, since the main centre of fell running was in the Lake District.' So Broderick, who in the early 1970s was 'deep into matters Celtic', introduced a Gaelic theme into the proceedings that endures today. 'I had a piper play at the start and the finish of the race. A presentation was made by Reverend Donald MacDonald, a native of Scarp and therefore a Gaelic speaker, which was followed by a ceilidh.'

A Navy vessel was anchored off Jura on July 14, 1973, the day of the inaugural race and six cadets were entered by the ship's captain, who said the exercise would do the men good. Of the 32 runners who started the race, 18 finished, with Bobby Shields of Clydebank Harriers winning in three hours and 56 minutes. None of the cadets made it to the finish line – two quit before they had even reached the first summit and the remaining four dropped out after Aonach-bheinn. The race was held again in 1974 and 1975, but was discontinued the following year when just six athletes entered. Broderick admitted: 'I was somewhat relieved, as it meant the disappearance of a foreign concept on Jura soil.' The race was eventually brought back in 1983 by Donald Booth, one of the cohort who first raced across the Paps a decade earlier. 'And what did you think of it?' Broderick asked.

'Hard,' I said wearily, exhaling loudly after the word as if to accentuate its meaning. 'One of the hardest races I've ever done. Pain and suffering, I think that sums it up.'

Broderick looked pleased. 'I'm proud of that,' he chuckled, 'one really has to suffer to understand the ecstasy of the race.'

7

Mull

The island of Mull, the magnificent isle,
the island of sun encompassed by the sea.
Island of triumph of the cold mountains
of the green woods and of desolate pastures.

Dugail MacPhàil

⌘

Twenty-four hours on Mull. What to do? It was already too late to reach Iona, the cradle of Christianity in Scotland. Lack of time ruled out any notion of visiting Gometra, Staffa or Ulva, Mull's other prominent island satellites. I did not have the inclination to climb Ben More, the western-most Munro. And I had seen enough whisky distilleries; I did not need to add Tobermory to my list.

My thoughts were still unresolved as I disembarked a ferry at Craignure, proceeding along a covered walkway to the shore. On the walls of the passage were images of the wildlife abounding on and around Mull: dolphins, por-poises, seals, sharks and whales in the seas; Arctic tern, eider duck, oyster catcher, puffin and razorbill in the skies. Next to each image was a list of facts about the creature: what it ate, where it lived, its lifespan and diet, any distinguishing or unusual traits, how and where it could be spotted. I was enthralled. That is it, I thought. That is what I will do on Mull: go on safari.

*

Such is the glorious assortment of wildlife on Mull, a report that a live but exhausted polar bear had been washed up on the island's shore was not inconceivable. Dave Sexton, an RSPB officer on Mull, said he had 'the shock of his life' when he made the discovery – the first non-captive polar bear to set paw on British land for 10,000 years.

'We rounded a headland on the west coast of the island and saw a large, white shape lying by some rocks in the distance. As we got closer, I was staggered to see that it was a polar bear. At first I felt sure it was dead, but then I realised it was still breathing. Scarily, it opened its eyes as we got next to it, but didn't show any other signs of moving.'

Sexton posed next to the bear, lying docile and on its belly on the tide line, for photographs, speculating the animal may have drifted to Mull on an ice floe from either Greenland or Svalbard.

The officer left the bear to get help, only to return an hour later to find the creature gone: a polar bear was loose on Mull.

'The coastguard, police and Arctic marine mammal experts are now searching for the animal. The public have been warned not to approach the bear if they see it, as it may be hungry after its long journey,' the RSPB informed the media.

Not long after, another press release was issued. The search was successful; the polar bear had been found, Sexton reported. 'The bear was so pleased to see me again, it rolled over and let me tickle its tummy.'

The story was an April fool's joke. The best of these are the ones people want to believe, and I desperately wanted to believe a polar bear had been washed up on Mull. For those who had not twigged, the tummy-tickling incident would have given the hoax away – although not for everyone. The following day, the *Independent* revealed that upon seeing the story, one of its environment correspondents scurried to his news desk in a flurry of excitement. No doubt, some seen-it-all-before news editor would have pointed to the date, bringing the enlivened reporter back down to Earth.

I was fortunate even to be on Mull, the second largest island of the Inner Hebrides. I had been nearing the end of a coach journey to Oban from Fort William when I fell into a deep slumber, waking to discover a new set of passengers boarding the vehicle. I hurried off, squeezing urgently past the embarking travellers. My bag – safely deposited in the luggage compartment of the coach in Fort William two hours earlier – was gone. I frantically scanned the ground in the immediate area, eyeing every passer-by with profound suspicion. Luckless, I extended my search, gazing up and down the road until I spotted the bag sitting on the edge of a pavement about fifty metres away. A wave of blessed relief swept through me. I crossed the road and wandered up to the bag, hoisting it onto my shoulders, as if this is exactly what I had always intended to do. The coach driver had obviously emptied the compartment of baggage and driven around the block, before parking at a different stance to pick up the fresh group of passengers. As if I were a sleeping child, neither he nor anyone else thought fit to wake me. Two minutes longer snoozing and I would have been on my way back to Fort William.

The colour-washed buildings on the Tobermory seafront are one of the iconic images of the Hebrides. Even the lime-green sign of the Co-op did not look out of place among the shades of blue, pink, red, white and yellow, which are reflected in the harbour waters. The Main Street backdrop was used as the setting of *Balamory*, a children's television programme that gave the world the infuriatingly catchy – unless you are under the age of five – song lines: 'What's the story in Balamory? Wouldn't you like to know?'

All was tranquil: the harbour water still and shimmering, the sun shining, the air scented with fish and chips and whisky. The hands on a clock tower were 15 minutes slow; on a day like today, it did not matter what the time was. The Hebridean saying: 'When God made time, he made plenty of it,' had rarely seemed more appropriate.

Posters advertising wildlife cruises and walks proliferated in Tobermory. Each time I turned a corner, an image of a grinning dolphin or a forlorn seal pup would be gazing back at me. The tours promised to reveal glimpses of an abundance of land and sea creatures: Arctic skua, dolphin, gannet, golden and white-tailed eagles, harbour porpoise, manx shearwater, minke whale, the 'mischievous' otter (why are human characteristics so often associated with an otter? Are they really mischievous or just going about their daily business, doing what otters do?), puffin and seal.

Wildlife tourism is big business in Scotland. A report published by the Scottish Government in 2010 calculated the industry is worth an estimated £65 million to the country's economy every year, sustaining the equivalent of 2,760 jobs. The study found that more than a million trips are made annually to Scotland by people whose main purpose is to view wildlife. Tourism associated with sea eagles is thought to generate about £2 million each year for the Mull economy alone. The so-called '*Springwatch* factor' was identified as one of the catalysts responsible for the boom in the wildlife tourism industry, with viewers of the BBC nature programmes *Springwatch* and *Autumnwatch* wowed by the spectacular footage of creatures in their natural habitats, including sea eagles on Mull and red deer on Rum.

'Post-Springwatchers are identified by many operators as individuals whose interest in wildlife has been kindled, or rekindled, by the media, and in particular popular television wildlife programmes,' the report explained. A survey carried out for the study, meanwhile, showed that almost a third of all wildlife-seekers were prompted to make the visit after being inspired by a radio or television programme.

I have no doubt the tours leaving from Tobermory deliver what they pledge, but signing up to one seemed akin to cheating. I wanted to observe Scotland's wildlife without having to go on a two-hour boat trip and without having to pay for the privilege. Like camping, swimming or walking in the wild, I felt it was my right to be able to set eyes on our native birds and mammals in their natural habitat. Granted, I knew it would not be easy. The brilliance of the camera-work on programmes such as *Springwatch* gives an un-realistic impression of how close one can physically get to a feral creature. I was unlikely to see a pod of whales serenading the Kilchoan-Tobermory ferry, for instance, or a turmoil of porpoises ordering fish suppers from the take-away van on the pier, but surely it could not be that hard? This was Mull after all, an island famed for its natural history – if not its polar bears.

Wildlife had always been a source of no more than mild curiosity to me. I had never owned a pair of binoculars. If I saw a wild creature in its natural environment, I saw it by chance, not design. It did not help that I was an ill-fated wildlife-spotter. At least it felt like that. In 18 months of living in the north of Scotland, I had only ever seen dolphins and seals once: dolphins from Chanonry Point on the Moray Firth, and seals – scores of them – languishing on the beaches of Findhorn Bay on the Moray coast. During my first prolonged period of time in Scotland, cycling along the Caithness and Sutherland coasts, it took me close to a week to spy my first deer.

My poor fortune was almost certainly to be blamed on ignorance. I am an awful birdwatcher, clueless about the teeming life in our seas. I do not know an Arctic skua from an Arctic tern. I have regularly been in the domain of the golden eagle, but have never seen one. Something that has a two-and-a-half metre wingspan is hard to miss. I am sure I have witnessed the flight of cormorant, eider duck and guillemot, but there was no way I could distinguish one from the other. I had, however, scored one noteworthy triumph on my island journey. I had established, conclusively and without a shred of doubt, what an oyster catcher was. It had happened as I walked along a spit of land to a ruined castle overlooking Loch Ranza on Arran. The wading bird may be easily identifiable by its long orange bill, black and white body and noisy shriek, but, for me, it was a wildlife epiphany. I realised for the first time the unexpected satisfaction one can gain from simply being able to positively identify a creature in the wild; it warmed my heart.

I walked along Main Street, passing a lifeboat station and ferry terminal, keeping my eyes focused on the sea. How difficult could it be? I asked myself again. Seals are common as rabbits, only they live in the sea. And why is a harbour porpoise so-called. Because they reside in harbours. And where am I? A harbour. Ahead was a bird that gave the impression of importance, strutting purposefully across the flat roof of the tourist information centre. A manx shearwater perhaps? A guillemot? Too small to be an eagle. I put on my glasses to sharpen the image. It was a seagull. Black-headed, herring, lesser black-backed or greater black-back? Even that was a seemingly unsolvable mystery.

I left the village, continuing on a coastal path, walking for about a mile-and-a-half to reach Rubha nan Gall lighthouse. From a stone memorial close to the building, there is a magnificent view across the junction of the Sound of Mull and Loch Sunart. Beyond the sea, the grassy slopes of Ben Hiant on Ardnamurchan dominated the spectacle, with the highest tops of the Rum Cuillin peering over the shoulder of the peninsula, mainland Scotland's westernmost land. There was no wildlife to be seen in the sea. No bobbing black heads, no dorsal fins breaking the surface. The occasional bird swept overhead and low across the sound, but they were too far away for me to see clearly. More seagulls in all likelihood.

I relocated, taking up a spot on a rocky beach north of the lighthouse, looking out into Bloody Bay, the scene of a 15th century naval battle between John, the last Lord of the Isles, and his son, Angus, who vanquished his father. I sat on the foreshore, waiting patiently. My senses were heightened, ears straining for unusual cries and sounds, eyes scouring the water for anything other than waves and white horses. Otters have apparently been spotted here. Not today. I saw only oyster catchers, bloody oyster catchers – I was bored of them now. I gave up after half an hour, wandering back to Tobermory. Knowing my luck, while I had been away I had missed a troupe of dolphins staging a synchronised swimming display in the harbour, accompanied by a killer whale blasting jets of water from its blowhole. As I wandered down Main Street, cute seals stared from billboards, taunting me.

There is of course a native Scottish creature that can be thoroughly relied upon, one that I have no difficulty in locating – the midge. My campsite was a further 20-minute, uphill walk from Tobermory, but when I returned I was pleasantly surprised – shocked even – to find the place midge-free. The location of the camping ground next to a 'picturesque burn' – so went the commercial blurb for the site – was a recipe for disaster, as was the stillness of the evening air. But midges are clever bastards. They lull their victims into a false sense of security, so much so I had gone as far as pulling my sleeping mattress from the tent and was preparing to read and write in the open air. In hindsight, it was madness. I had scanned a single paragraph only when I sensed a buzzing close to my left ear. I looked up to see a few blood-suckers flitting about me, then a few more, then a lot more. The midges seemed to be breeding in midair, regenerating like some unbeatable mutant army. Before I had even considered applying repellent, it was too late. They had won. I retreated to my tent.

The site boasted of having two midge-trapping machines. They work by releasing carbon dioxide – the gas that attracts the insects to humans – and subsequently sucking them, in enormous quantities, into a net where they die. The machine targets the biting, egg-laying female midge. The owner of the site countered this technology by warning: 'We are not guaranteeing midge-free camping, but they do catch a huge number.' Whether the midge magnets were on or off, working or not, there seemed to be a 'huge number' – several billion apparently – that appeared immune to magnetisation. Midge magnets? A valiant attempt, but a nuclear holocaust would not see off the little blighters.

My failure ever to pitch a tent on a flat piece of land persisted, causing me to wake every hour to peel a cheek off the side of the flysheet. With my time on Mull fast expiring, I had one last wildlife-hunting throw of the dice. I ran west on the road to Dervaig, expecting nothing, seeing nothing. I stopped a couple with binoculars and asked what they were looking at or for. They shook their heads. They were French and did not understand what I was asking. They could have spotted a woolly mammoth grazing by the

Tobermory River for all I knew. Running back to the campsite, I mulled over the words of the saying: 'The more you look, the less you see.' They had taken on a new resonance.

My 24 hours on Mull were almost over; I had failed in my task. I caught a bus south to Craignure, nursing a disquiet that I had missed much on the island. Not just the wildlife, but its northern, western and southern shores, the wild Ross of Mull, Fingal's Cave on Staffa, the abbey on Iona, the ruined chapel on Inchkenneth. It was a long list. Still, as fulfilling as it can be to exhaust a place, it is also satisfying to have a reason to return.

8

Coll

Col is not properly rocky; it is rather one continued rock, of a surface much diversified with protuberances, and covered with a thin layer of earth, which is often broken, and discovers the stone.

Samuel Johnson

⌘

James Boswell and Samuel Johnson came to Coll by accident in 1773, driven to the island by a ferocious storm when their destination upon leaving the Skye port of Armadale had been Mull. Recalling the dreadful happenings aboard their ship, a seasick Johnson wrote: 'We were doomed to experience, like others, the danger of trusting to the wind, which blew against us, in a short time, with such violence, that we, being no seasoned sailors, were willing to call it a tempest.'

While Johnson retreated to his bunk, Boswell stayed on deck, fearing the ship would be sunk. 'I saw tonight what I never saw before,' he wrote, 'a prodigious sea with immense billows coming upon a vessel, so as that it seemed hardly possible to escape. There was something grandly horrible in the sight. I am glad I have seen it once.'

The vessel carrying Boswell, a 37-year-old lowland Scotsman, and Johnson, a 64-year-old Englishman, passed by Eigg and Muck, with the storm worsening as they navigated rough sea off Ardnamurchan. Unable to enter the Sound of Mull, the ship's skipper set a course for Coll, declaring:

'Let us run for it, in God's name.' Boswell, meanwhile, prayed for his life. 'I was really in very great fear this night,' he admitted after.

The prayers of Boswell were answered: the ship escaped the fury of the storm, casting anchor off Coll. The literary travellers went ashore the next day 'in prodigious rain', the first of eleven unplanned days on the island. Journeying across Coll, the conversations, eccentricities and observations they fastidiously recorded would later be published in their respective diaries, Boswell's *Journal of a Tour to the Hebrides*, and Johnson's *Journey to the Western Islands of Scotland*.

My expedition to Coll was a rather more straightforward affair: a three-hour ferry journey from Oban on a breezy, fair May afternoon. As we neared a pier, extending from the western entrance of Loch Eatharna, I glimpsed a large, black outline beneath the surface of the water, no more than 50 metres away. The shape came nearer, moving on a parallel course to the ship. The outline broke the surface: a broad, glossy back appearing, then a dorsal fin rose majestically. It was a minke whale. I was starstruck, giddy with excitement. I tapped the shoulder of a woman standing next to me, pointing a finger towards the great mammal. We watched together transfixed, mesmerised by this creature from the deep, glorying in its size and sudden appearance.

Without moving her eyes from the whale, the woman told me she and her husband were returning to Coll forty years after their first and last time here. She recalled sunny days, wild camping, walks along crystal shores lapped by cobalt seas, adventure. Her husband moved behind her, putting his arms around his wife. She turned to smile, lovingly and happily, at him, and for an intimate moment I was utterly shut out of their existence. I was alone. In that instant I missed Fi terribly; I recalled the contentment of shared experiences, of moments like these, sharing life. Sharp but momentary, the anguish was replaced by a dull, hollow ache. Perhaps Christopher McCandless, the young American who died on his own while attempting to live off the land in Alaska, was right when during his final days he wrote: 'Happiness only real when shared.'

First impressions are everything, and whether it was the revelatory sight of the whale or some invisible, magical force, I felt instantly at ease on Coll. Leaving the hubbub of the ferry terminal, I wandered up a single-track road towards the white-washed cottages of Arinagour, marvelling at my new surroundings. By way of an introduction to the island, a tourist pamphlet produced by Coll businesses, the RSPB and Scottish Natural Heritage states on its first page: 'Welcome to Coll. Firstly, slow down. What's the rush? You've got time to unwind, you've escaped . . .' My eyes would normally skim over such words, deriding them as tourist hogwash. One word in particular struck a profound chord – escape. That is how I felt – as if I had escaped. Coll seemed to belong to another realm, one that exuded possibilities.

Rain began falling shortly before dawn. A keen wind billowed through the tent, causing the canvas to quiver back and forth. I had not walked far the previous night, camping on rough grazing land above the Coll Hotel. Discarded beer bottles and round patches of scorched earth indicated I was not the first person to make this a temporary home. There had been one other camper, a chain-smoking teacher in his late 50s who had only a bivouac bag for shelter. My accommodation, however cramped, was palatial in comparison to his coffin-like contraption.

I read for an hour before cooking breakfast. I ate slowly, chewing deliberately, drawing out time. The sickly sweetness of the syrup in my porridge made me retch, intensifying

my desire to break free of the confines of my tent. Rain
continued to hammer the walls, incessant but mercifully no
tempest. I lay very still, imagining the pace of the drops
slowing, only for the pitter-patter to accelerate. Rain always
sounds worse inside the tent, was my well-worn mantra.
Another hour slipped past, by which time I was convinced
the downpour really had eased. I poked my head out,
swivelling it sideways to inspect the wide Hebridean sky.
The clouds were surprisingly high and light. The western
firmament was brightening, making me wonder where the
deluge was coming from. A lamb surveying my actions from
a few metres away suddenly emitted a series of shrill,
alarmed baas. The noise alerted its mother, who flashed
a filthy look in my direction. The lamb slowly backed away
to a safe distance, shaking its head dubiously, as if to say:
'Rain's set in. Stay where you are if I were you.'

Ignoring the best intentions of the lamb, I pulled on
waterproofs and headed down a rocky track that led to
the village shop. Walking the same route the previous
evening, I had asked a man in the first house I had come
to about my chances of hitchhiking around the island. I
would undoubtedly get a lift, plenty of lifts, he assured me,
but offered to give me a bicycle instead. As Coll measures
13 miles from top to tip and is no broader than four miles,
a bicycle was the ideal mode of transport on which to
explore it.

'If there's one in the garage, I'll leave it by the gate,' he
had said. True to his word, a snazzy blue and yellow
mountain bike, with an equally snazzy name, Raleigh
Vulture, was leaning against the fence outside his home.

The rain had halted, but as I set out on the cross-island
road to Coll's west coast I kept my waterproofs on, so as
not to tempt fate. Progress was slow. Snazzy from a distance, the bike was close to being a write-off. There were no

rear brakes, the crank made a persistent groan, the gears rattled up and down the cogs, a number of spokes were loose and the tires needed blowing up. In the bike's defence, the suspension worked admirably. I had scarcely travelled a mile when I pulled over to permit an oncoming motorist to cross a cattle grid. The driver stopped, winding down the window. It was the man who had loaned me the bike.

'How is it?'

'Brilliant,' I said enthusiastically.

'Bit of a problem with the brakes, I reckon.'

'Really?' I hadn't noticed. 'Ah yes,' I said, pulling the brake lever and gesturing towards the rear wheel, 'the back ones don't seem to work.'

I reached a junction some minutes later. This was Arnabost, where a right turn takes the traveller to the dead-end of Sorisdale, a hamlet abandoned during the Clearances, and a left turn leads to Ballyhaugh, another cul-de-sac, beyond which is the splendid Hogh Bay. I went right, climbing steeply for a short time and then freewheeling down to a burial ground at Kilyinaik, the northerly extent of the tour of Coll made by Boswell and Johnson. I amused myself by picturing how Johnson, with a frame described by Boswell as 'gigantic and grown unwieldy from corpulence' would appear on a bicycle. I imagined him wobbling clumsily across the road, cursing the machine and throwing it into the dunes as he faltered on an undulation.

Boswell wrote of seeing the 'ruins of a church or chapel . . . beside which was a place of graves.' The map identified a burial ground and the remains of a church, with the landmarks standing on opposite sides of the road. Which one Boswell spoke of, I could not be sure. The burial ground, oblong in shape, on the coastal side of the road was easy to find. It was surrounded by fence and split into two parts: the old, containing headstones that post-dated

Boswell and Johnson by more than a century, and the new, where memorials for several unnamed World War II sailors stood. I ventured across the road in search of the remains of the church. It was a fruitless hunt. A large stone pen for animals seemed to stand on the spot where the church was marked on the map. Perhaps the walls of the church were used in the construction of the pen? Or, more likely, I was simply looking in the wrong place.

I retrieved the bike and cycled the way I had come, returning to Arnabost and continuing southward to Bally-haugh on a route flanked by yellow-flowering flag iris. Bulky Ben Hogh, Coll's 106-metre highest point, domi-nated the view in front. Clearly visible from the road was a large boulder close to the hill's summit, said to have been thrown to its lofty position by a giant aiming for his mistress. Legend says the mistress hurled a stone down at the giant in retaliation. 'It was all in sport,' Boswell reckoned. I left the bike propped outside the Hebridean Centre, the headquarters of the Project Trust, a gap year charity, at Ballyhaugh, and skirted a small loch to reach the ramparts of Ben Hogh.

The giant's stone was exactly as described by Boswell: 'It is clearly detached from the earth or any rock. The top of the hill is rocky, but it is supported upon three stones of no great size.' He went on: 'There is all the appearance that it has been set up artificially; yet it is difficult to conceive how it has been done.' I marvelled at the stone. It was like a magic trick, a massive weight supported by mere pebbles. Johnson did not climb Ben Hogh, preferring to sit and read a book on the hill's lower slopes. I lingered for some time on the summit. The leaden morning skies were gradually being replaced by a vivid blue. The clouds carrying the morning rain were charging east. The view was inspirational: the southern islands of the Western Isles, Canna, Rum, Eigg,

Skye, Mull, the Treshnish Isles, the unmistakable Paps on Jura, Gunna and Tiree, the two islands south of Coll, as well as numerous others I could not positively identify. Coll possessed the twin quality of being peripheral, on the edge, yet also central and surrounded by islands.

Although the road ended at the Hebridean Centre, I was able to continue my cycling journey on a track that criss-crossed dunes behind Hogh Bay, joining another road at Totronald. I had not been on the road long when I came to Na Sgeulachan, a pair of triangular standing stones in a field of swaying grass and buttercups positioned some 15 metres apart. Dating back to 2500BC, the flagstones are Coll's earliest recorded monuments. The wires of an electricity pylon now cross the land. Legend says two ogres or ogre's children are buried between the stones, with each headstone marking a grave. Alternatively, the stones may mark the graves of the boulder-tossing giant and his mistress. A group of birdwatchers on an RSPB tour endeavouring to see corncrakes, a rare bird that arrives on Coll in April after wintering in south-east Africa, were standing nearby, binoculars pointed into the distance. Making its nest in long grass, the corncrake is a difficult bird to spot, and the group did not seem to be having much success.

Boswell said the stones were 'probably' the remains of a Druidic temple and went on to recount a trick that can be played on a stranger: 'He is desired to lie down behind the easternmost one (or the westernmost, according to the route he is on) and told that he will hear everything that is said by the company, who stand at the other stone; and while he is lying in patient attention, the company get off and leave him; and when he at last gets up, he finds himself all alone.' Perhaps I cannot grasp the nuances of 18th century humour, but the more I re-read the account the more confused I become. What is the joke?

The road dropped to the shimmering sea-inlet of Loch Breachacha, passing a small airfield – Coll's aerial link to the world beyond its shores. There are two castles at Breachacha, a name that translates charmingly from Gaelic as the field speckled with wild-flowers. The newest of the castles – now a family home – was built in the 1750s, shortly before Boswell and Johnson came to stay. Boswell said the pair were at first 'very comfortable', but later described the mansion as 'a tradesman's box' and 'a kind of waste house'. Standing 'two gun-shots' away, the older and smaller of the castles, dating back to the 15th century, was an imposing building, its grim exterior reminding me of a Moroccan mud fortress. Built on a low rocky prow at the head of Loch Breachacha, the prison-like nature of the castle was redeemed by an exquisite view from its upper windows. Beyond the castle was the deserted, white-sand shore of Breachacha Bay, washed by a sparkling sea. I waded into silky, warm water, reaching an offshore sand-bank, stepping from thigh-deep sea to ankle-deep. As I paddled on my own private beach, a plane I had not seen approaching from the east swooped overhead, momentarily shattering the illusion of magic on the island of Coll. I heard the wheels touch down on the runway and the plane come to a halt. Peace pervaded Coll once again.

As on Colonsay, I fell into an easy habit of discovering an extraordinary beach, only to stumble across an even more extraordinary one a short while later. This time Breachacha Bay was surpassed by Crossapol Bay. I cycled unhurriedly along the shoreline of the new beach, slowing and almost falling off when softer sand caused the tires to sink and drag. The sun now glared from a bright sky. Boswell and Johnson also came here, riding along the beach on horse-back, with the former calling the bay a 'fine strand' and an 'admirable airing ground'. Leaving the bike, I continued on foot along a path that meandered across sand dunes, marram grass tickling my calves, until I reached a cemetery at Crossapol. The burial site was 'closed', according to a sign erected by Argyll and Bute Council. Ancient, doubled over and weathered, many of the graves belonged to the Macleans of Coll, chieftains of the island for half a millennium. Each headstone faced away from the land, looking over a glinting sea to Mull – a final resting place of such magnificence it would calm the most restless of souls.

By the time I had retraced my steps to where I had jettisoned the bike, a herd of cows had invaded the beach. Half a dozen calves were dipping their hooves in the sea, while a large black cow shattered the silence with a chorus of rowdy moos. The herd began to mooch deliberately along the shore towards Crossapol, as if this was nothing out of the ordinary, a typical afternoon outing for the group.

I have an unfounded suspicion of cows. Fond of looking at them from the safety of the other side of a fence, without a barrier between us I find the animals too big and too unpredictable to trust. Keen to reach Feall Bay on the west side of the island, I re-entered the dunes, this time lugging the bike alongside me, giving the cows a wide berth. I thought I had eluded them, only to turn a corner to see a queue of the beasts ahead. One turned her head towards me, staring in horror and then releasing a startled grunt that sent cows scattering in various directions across the dunes.

The bays of Crossapol and Feall are separated by a mile-wide wilderness of marram dunes, a puzzling place of rolling sand mounds. I strained to hear the sound of waves breaking on the western shore; the uniformity of the surroundings meant I must rely only on my ears to guide me to

Feall Bay. Once in the interior of the wilderness, without the guidance of the sun I would not have known north from south, east from west. Boswell and Johnson had a similarly confusing passage through this sandy maze as they sought the remains of houses that had been blown over by sand. 'This led us a strange zigzag journey among the sand-hills,' Boswell wrote. 'There was a good deal of wind, and good deal of sand was thrown in our faces. I cried, "This is quite Arabian".'

A head-high fence, presumably to hem in the cows, blocked my way, extending as far as I could see left and right. I heaved the bike up and over, and then clambered onto the other side myself, snagging shorts on the wire. The roar of the waves was growing louder, but the sea remained hidden behind peaks of sand. I found myself on a snaking path of sand so narrow I had to drag the bike clumsily behind me. A foot was swallowed by a hidden hole, causing my weight to be thrown forward, sending me flailing to the ground. The bike came crashing down on top of me, the rusty jaws of the chain rings taking a chomp out of an ankle. I hobbled on, blood dripping from the wound.

The dunes seemed endless. I climbed steeply to the lid of the tallest so far, expecting to see hundreds more unfurled before me. There were none: only the tremendous sweep of Feall Bay. I gazed up and down the empty beach, shaking my head with disbelief. As impossible as the notion seemed, here was a beach more extraordinary than the two extraordinary beaches preceding it. Boswell too believed Feall – or Foill, as he called it, was a more splendid sight than Crossapol, calling the west beach a 'very good airing strand'. Boswell's words were a gross understatement; Feall Bay was the finest airing stand I had yet seen on the islands of the Firth of Clyde and the Hebrides.

I bathed my bleeding ankle in the Atlantic, before sauntering bare-foot along the beach, the only person, it seemed, on the planet. A village had stood at the northern end of the beach at the time of Boswell and Johnson's visit, with the former counting 'so many houses'. I saw none, nor any indication that anyone could have ever lived here. Even in 1773, when the population stood at around 700, Boswell described the island as 'very populous'. Coll's population once numbered the many hundreds, peaking at 1442 people living in 271 houses in the mid-19th century. It was hard to imagine how so many people fitted onto such a small island. The then laird, Maclean, agreed. The island could not support the population, he said, and cleared half the inhabitants to Australia. By 1881 the population had dipped to 643, plummeting ever since and now standing at about 150.

My musings during the last six miles of cycling on an increasingly rickety mount were dominated by food. The options for dining out were limited. There was a café and a hotel, both of which were in Arinagour. Islanders on Coll (and also on Tiree), however, have found an unusual way to get around their slim culinary pickings. They order a long-distance takeaway – from a restaurant on Barra, the mere matter of a 50-mile sea journey away. Ordering their meal on the day a ferry is due to sail from the Barra port of Castlebay to the Inner Hebrides, Barra lamb bhoona, Minch prawn jaipuri and scallop pakora are delivered to waiting islanders on the piers of Coll and Tiree.

Once in Arinagour, my choice was limited further. The café being shut, it was the Coll Hotel or nothing. I perused the menu, deliberating which dish might be the largest, before narrowing down the options to which might be the largest at the cheapest price. It would be rude to go down this line of questioning in a respectable establishment, but over the years I have carefully honed my tactics, using what

I call the I-have-not-eaten-all-day approach, rather than admitting I am a voracious cheapskate.

'The prawns – is that a big dish?' I queried a server.

He was a man after my own heart, soon cottoning on to the connotation of my words. He shook his head.

'Fish and chips?' I tried. When is fish and chips not a sizeable portion, I thought.

'That big,' the server said, extending his hands to demonstrate the size of the plate, while shaking his head again. 'The duck is a big portion.'

'I'm not keen on duck,' I said, lying. It was the price I was not keen on.

'The steak?' Same problem.

I plumped for the half-way house – chicken and haggis in a whisky sauce, a generously-portioned meal but cheaper than the duck or steak.

I am a great advocate of the morale-boosting powers of food, of the qualitative and quantitative effect of eating. I strode out of the Coll Hotel that night with a spring in my step, a man rejuvenated.

I woke early, sleeping soundly and undisturbed for the first time in nearly a week. Feeling sprightly, I ran the route I had cycled the previous day, to Arnabost and then to the top of the steep hill above Kilyinaik, before returning the same way and sprinting the final half-mile. My relationship with porridge at breaking point, I instead ate boiled eggs with bread soaked in olive oil. After hurriedly packing up, I scurried through Arinagour to meet a morning ferry.

My time on Coll had been a whirlwind romance. Less than 48 hours earlier, the island had been a stranger. In that time its rugged interior, pockmarked by lochans, and its sandy fringes had beguiled and transfixed me. I wanted to stay for ever. Coll was part of me, under my skin. I could scarcely live without her. She was incomparable.

Johnson did not agree; the island failed to win him over. Coll was not visited often, he said, because 'there is not much to amuse curiosity or to attract avarice'. Writing about the fifth day of their stay on Coll, Boswell recalled 'He (Johnson) felt today of the weight of this barren way of passing time. He said: "I want to be on the mainland, and go on with existence. This is a waste of a life".'

Boswell's appreciation for Coll reached greater heights. Remembering a conversation with Johnson while on the island, the Englishman said it would require 'great resignation to live on one of these islands'.

'I don't know,' Boswell had retorted, 'I have felt myself at times in a state of almost physical existence, satisfied to eat, drink and sleep, and walk about and enjoy my own thoughts; and I can figure a continuation of this.'

'Ay sir,' said he; 'but if you were shut up here, your own thoughts would torment you; you would think of Edinburgh or London, and that you could not be there.'

I could, almost, understand Johnson's way of thinking – to some people islands are paradises, to others they are prisons. Coll made Johnson feel trapped. The island made me feel free. The joy of Coll comes from its deficiencies and difficulties – the lack of a proper path through the sand dunes between Crossapol and Feall bays, the absence of anywhere to buy food outside Arinagour, the scrap of rough ground that counts as a campsite. There is so much pleasure in simplicity, in being able to step away from the confusion of western living without actually leaving the shores of the UK.

The island needs no fancy slogans, no gimmicks; the charms of Coll stem from what it lacks. A community-run website, Visit Coll, goes as far as admitting that 'there is almost nowhere to stay and nothing to do once here'. Bemoaning travellers who demand 'every mainland convenience', the 'about Coll' section gives a frank health warning to those considering holidaying on the island: 'Coll has, for example, no visitor points, no tourist information, no interpretation panels to ruin the environment, no mobile phone coverage (except a few spots, and then only sometimes), no public transport of any sort, no MacDonald's, no Tesco or Apple Store (and may it remain that way), no policeman, no street lights, no parking meters, the worst road surfaces you are likely to find in the UK, the most expensive diesel and petrol in the UK (maxed at £1.60 per litre in 2009!), and often nowhere to go whilst it rains.'

Boswell and a relieved Johnson left lovely Coll for Mull on a boat taking in kelp. I took a ferry to Tiree.

9

Tiree

The Land below Sea-Level, surrounded by rough waves,
the famous, valuable island;
The sea resounds constantly as it pounds it;
It is now known as Tiree.

John MacLean

❧

'Shark,' a cry went up from the port deck. There were two of them, their fins slicing menacingly through the dark water between the ship and Tiree. Passengers surged to the railings encircling the deck, with those who had seen the sharks pointing animatedly at the black triangles to guide those who had not. 'Basking sharks', a bearded, anorak-clad man surmised, observing the big fish through binoculars. Moving in the opposite direction to the ferry, they crossed the white, churning water of our wake, setting a course for Mull. A minute later, there was another cry, this time from the starboard deck, where a single dorsal fin, mysterious and threatening, trailed the others.

Seen from the sea, Tiree would win no beauty contest. But then nor would Coll, which rises barren and ostensibly vacant. Tiriodh, the Gaelic name for Tiree, loosely translates as the low land of barley or corn – an indicator of its fertile soils – but the island is also known descriptively as the land below the waves. Sailing into Gott Bay, as St Columba once did, with his boat striking a rock and almost sinking, the traveller soon recognises why. Apart from three obvious protrusions in the far west, of which radar station-topped Ben Hynish is the highest, Tiree is flat and low-lying. Faced with a tsunami, the island would put up little resistance.

Coll and Tiree are frequently uttered in the same breath. The islands are like identical sisters, similarly sized (Tiree is marginally larger), similarly placed, similarly constructed, and even once conjoined. But Tiree, the westernmost of the Inner Hebrides, is the dominant sibling, better-known and better-serviced. They are unequal relations. The 800 permanent inhabitants of Tiree outnumber Collachs five-to-one. Tiree has a high school; the children of secondary age on Coll are educated at a school in Oban – 45 miles away. Blessed with fertile soils, Tiree is agriculturally-rich; wrapped in peat bog and rock, Coll is not. And unlike Coll, Tiree's community website does not warn potential visitors that there is 'nothing to do'. Taking a rather more proactive approach to tourism than its Inner Hebridean neighbour, the Tiree website declares: 'If you seek tranquillity, freedom of space and clean pure air, the isle of Tiree has it all.' Coll is even overlooked in song.

> The boat leaves Oban every day,
> Passing Tobermory on the way,
> Onwards to the lovely isle of Coll,
> To Tiree, the most beautiful of all.

As with any siblings, Coll and Tiree are contrasting personalities. Once on land, Tiree unhesitatingly thrust her charms at me, parading her obvious beauty. Tiree was flaunting and promiscuous. Coll had been reluctant and shy. Tiree gave herself up easily, spreading her handsome adornments on a plate. Coll had demanded to be wined and dined. Within minutes of our first encounter,

Tiree had stripped off before me, nakedly displaying her alluring assets: white beaches, azure waters and pretty machair. Coll possesses similar glories, but she keeps them hidden, secret – at least until the third or fourth date. Tiree provoked lust, Coll love.

I followed signposts from the ferry terminal to Scarinish, the largest settlement on Tiree, boasting an art gallery, bank, butcher, hotel, fire and police stations, museum, school and supermarket. The village was a metropolis in comparison to Arinagour. The supermarket faced onto a large telecommunications mast, behind which I pitched my tent, taking care to stay out of sight of houses.

Islanders are tolerant of wild camping. Not that they have any choice – it is legal, after all. Turn up in a campervan or motorhome, however, and one will find that the forbearance of islanders has worn thin. Tiree has become a victim of success. Not only is the island physically tempting, Tiree is reputed to be one the sunniest places in Britain, with the Gulf Stream keeping temperatures mild year-round. Stories of the island's beauty and pleasant climate have spread far and wide, across the UK and beyond. Holidaymakers in campervans and motorhomes came in their droves. Then, in 2008, the Scottish Government introduced the Road Equivalent Tariff, a two-and-a-half year pilot scheme pegging ferry fares to Coll, Tiree and the Western Isles, to the price of a road journey of comparative length. The cost of sea crossings tumbled as a consequence. High ferry prices were a drag on the economic progress of the Hebrides, the government argued.

So, inevitably, even more people came to Tiree. The number of campervans and motorhomes piling on to the island rose by 50 per cent in the first eight months of the pilot, then by 154 per cent in the next two months. The infrastructure of Tiree, although more advanced than on Coll, began to creak. The sheer number of visitors was causing damage to the island's chief assets – its dunes, grazing land and machair. Stirred into action, the people of Tiree seized the initiative.

On the journey to Tiree, a message relayed over the public-address system of MV *Clansman* had summoned those in charge of campervans and motorhomes to the ship's office to be issued with a guide to access, overnight parking and waste disposal on Tiree. Drivers – once accused of living in 'Never Never Land' because of their apparent disregard for machair – did as they were told, filing forward like naughty schoolchildren called to see the head teacher. Other passengers resisted the urge to boo and hiss in a pantomime-style at the baddies.

'Tiree has always welcomed visitors in motorhomes and campervans and there were rarely any problems in the past with these vehicles parking off-road and along the beaches,' the pamphlet starts. A but – a big but – was imminent, I could tell. 'Unfortunately, the large increase in numbers of these vehicles over the last two years has made a notable impact on the land. To protect the island's natural beauty and environment, the community of Tiree has come to-gether and through the (Tiree) Access Steering Group and in accordance with the Scottish Outdoor Access Code, has decided to put limitations on land use. These limitations have been introduced to protect the rights and livelihoods of the landowners, whilst improving the visitor experience and moving towards a more sustainable form of tourism.'

The access group set aside 14 designated sites – all of them on working crofts – for campervans and motorhomes, each providing two to three pitches and costing a 'very reasonable' £10 per night. The sites were spread across the island, from Kilkenneth in the west to Port Ban in the east. Specific areas for 'day parking' had also been reserved at three beaches. Now, rather than moseying wherever the wind takes them, and staying there overnight for free, new arrivals on Tiree are asked to report to a so-called 'access officer', who will 'arrange the booking for your overnight parking sites for the duration of your stay on the island'. The officious process rather shatters any romantic notions of a touring holiday in a campervan.

The policy has been created with the best of intentions: to protect the precious and pristine Tiree landscape, for this is the reason people come to the island. Yet in my mind, what the policy does not discuss is an underlying grievance against campervans and motorhomes, boiling down to one dirty, divisive word: money. In hard cash terms, what benefits do these tourists bring? How do they support the fragile economies of Tiree or any of the Hebridean islands? They clearly have no requirement for bed and breakfasts, guesthouses, hostels and hotels. They are likely to have stocked up their vehicles with food and provisions, negating the need to shop locally or eat out at cafés and restaurants. And they will almost certainly have filled fuel tanks to the brim in Glasgow, Inverness or Oban, rather than paying the sky-high prices at petrol stations on the Hebrides.

It is easy to generalise and hyperbolise (and I have), but theoretically, once a ferry fare has been expended, campervan and motorhome travellers can enjoy cost-free living on Tiree. Although, not any longer, of course. If the backcloth of Tiree is preserved and the birds, bumblebees and butterflies that rely on the machair are safeguarded, then surely the overnight fee – a stealth tax, it could be argued – is justified? The owners of campervans and motorhomes could present a dogged counter argument, I imagine. Why should they be forced to contribute to the economy of Tiree? They have spent thousands of pounds on a vehicle that enables self-sufficiency. Why should they be punished for making that choice? And these were straitened times of economic restraint and recession. Who would not only want to save money, but need to save money?

Tiree depends on crofting and tourism. Its future also depends on striking the right balance between the two.

I walked back through Scarinish, continuing along a road to a cluster of buildings at Gott. Every oncoming driver slowed and waved. Sheep roamed everywhere. Birds wheeled overhead, a squawking cacophony. I left the road and followed a track that meandered across machair, a swaying, yellow carpet of buttercups, before passing a series of little lochs to reach the northern fringe of Tiree. Machair on this rockier, wilder shore was even prettier, with daisies, flag iris, fluffy cotton grass and purple orchids, mingling with the ever-present buttercups. There were many more flowers I could not identify; up to 45 plant species can be recognised (not by me) in a typical square metre of machair.

Machair is found exclusively on the Atlantic fringes of Ireland and Scotland. South Uist arguably possesses the most impressive expanse in Scottish terms, with flowering pastures stretching along the entire length of its western seaboard, but the plains are also extensive on the coasts of the northern isles, elsewhere on the Western Isles, and on Coll and Tiree. The lime-rich soil of machair is created by sand containing alkaline seashells being blown ashore, neutralising the acid peat bogs on land. Green meadows during the winter, machair explodes into life in summertime, becoming a carpet of colour.

Machair is a little like Gaelic. Both are threatened with extinction and are limited to specific geographic locations – but people are still prepared to throw money at the causes. In the case of machair, the RSPB announced in 2009 it was to spend £2million on conserving the Hebridean meadows, announcing a scheme to financially reward crofters who desist from using chemicals and correlate grass-cutting and harvesting around the breeding patterns of birds. The significant outlay becomes understandable when the list of birds – some rare, some not so rare – that machair supports has been considered: corncrake, corn bunting, dunlin, greylag goose, lapwing, northern plover, oyster-catcher, redshank, sandpiper, skylark, snipe, tern, twite and whooper swan.

I was amused by machair. Not because the sight of machair is in anyway laugh out loud funny. But because of the reference Compton Mackenzie made to machair in his Scottish island-based comedy *Whisky Galore*. Sergeant-major Fred Odd, being English, cannot pronounce the word machair as an islander would, as hard as he tries. As Odd walks across the machair with his mother he describes the moment he told his sweetheart, Peggy Macroon, that he loved her.

'It was a lovely day the same as what it is now, and the macker was covered with daisies the same as what it is now.'

'Macker? What's that?'

'Macker's what they call all this grassy land. Garlic.'

I followed the rugged line of the shore east, coming to a large, flat-bottomed boulder marooned on a ledge of rock above a beach. The Ringing Stone was deposited on Tiree during the last Ice Age more than 10,000 years ago. The island is predominately made up of Lewisian gneiss, the oldest rocks in Britain, but the Ringing Stone was a much younger type of igneous rock, indicating it was an erratic, transported here from Rum by the power of glaciation.

The name must have relevance, I reasoned, and I set about trying to make the Ringing Stone ring. It seemed implausible. How can a rock ring? I tapped pebbles against the mighty boulder, listening for a noise. The sound created was one of clashing stones, nothing more, nothing unusual. I tried a larger rock, with the same result. I thought the ring may be something to do with an echo, so I lay flat on the ground and bawled at the base of the Ringing Stone. Still it did not ring. I sat down on the beach, scooping tiny shells and letting them run through my fingers, miffed at the stone's silence but awed by the 20-mile journey the erratic had travelled to perch on Tiree.

Just then I noticed two figures, a man and a woman, approaching from the machair, walking purposefully towards the Ringing Stone. I shuffled further away, hoping they had not been watching my pitiful efforts to play the boulder. The man was no more than half a dozen strides away when he stooped to pick up a rock from the beach, tossing it towards the top of the Ringing Stone. It sounded, an unmistakable tinny ring, not unlike that of a bell.

'Extraordinary isn't it?' the man said, turning to me.

'Sure is,' I muttered.

The couple fussed about the stone, taking photographs, running their hands across the pockmarked surface. Eventually they turned to the west, heading towards Balephetrish Bay, leaving me alone to test the phenomenon for myself. I carefully selected a large stone and took aim at the target. It sailed wildly wide of the rock, almost striking an unsuspecting seagull. I looked around, again to see if anyone was observing, burning with embarrassment. The Ringing Stone was making a mug of me. I hurled a second rock, a little too aggressively, for this is the oldest monument on Tiree, but the missile this time made a firm contact. It rang: music to my ears.

Then I rained stones on the rock – it rang and rang and rang.

The Ringing Stone is decorated by 53 circular and oval marks, pointing to the existence of a pre-Christian religion on Tiree. The indentations may represent the form of the female breast or could have been used to hold blood during sacrifices, a sign erected nearby as part of the 30-mile Tiree Pilgrimage Trail suggested. Beyond doubt is the symbolism the prehistoric population of Tiree must have attached to the unreal ringing of the rock. Folklore states the rock was hurled here from Mull by a giant, and should the Ringing Stone be removed or smashed the island below the waves actually will sink beneath the Atlantic surf.

I continued across machair, passing grazing cows and the remains of Dùn Mòr broch, a round, 1st century, fortification constructed on the summit of a rocky knoll, before reaching the hamlet of Vaul. A modest elevation here gave a fine view west across a pancake-flat interior, rising only at the outer edges. In such landscapes, the wideness of the sky is accentuated. Tiree is at its narrowest – a little more than half-a-mile – at Vaul, and cutting across the island to Ruaig I soon reacquainted myself with the softer, south side.

Traigh Mhòr, a grey-white vastness of sand, is Tiree's longest beach. The strip was forsaken, save for two kite surfers in wetsuits, one seemingly coaching the other on dry land, and the occasional dog-walker. The emptiness of the beach was at odds with what I expected from Tiree, the island dubbed 'the Hawaii of the north'. Type the words 'Tiree' and 'beaches' into an internet search engine and it will return hundreds of pictures of flawless, silver sands, more Seychelles than Scotland. So spectacular is the sand that there was a major outcry in 2010 after it emerged tonnes were being illegally pilfered from around the island's 46-mile coastline. The Hawaii parallel is a nod not only to

Tiree's beaches, but also to its reputation as a surfing – board, kite and wind – hotspot. The waves breaking on the island's west coast have been unhindered for 3000 miles. The Tiree Wave Classic for windsurfing was established on the crest of the island's burgeoning popularity for such diversions in 1986, and has grown into the premier event of its kind in the UK, taking place annually in October.

The day had become hazy and muggy, and as I trudged wearily across the everlasting and unchanging beach I longed to be back in Scarinish. Once there, I sprawled on the grass outside my tent door, staring across the sea to Mull. A wonderful spectacle to behold, particularly at nightfall when it became a silhouette, I preferred to admire Mull from afar than exist on Mull.

It was a good day to leave: low cloud and fine rain. Mull had disappeared. Earwigs had taken refuge in the clothes and food I had left outside, scurrying frantically for shelter when disturbed. I ate eggs again, unable to stomach porridge. I felt lethargic, extraordinarily tired. I longed to lie, comfortable and warm, in a world of restful sleep, but tents – certainly not my tent – are not conducive to such luxuries. My reflection in the mirror in the public toilets at Scarinish was ragged and shaggy, a poor advertisement for the rejuvenating powers of island living.

I packed up and made my way to the pier.

Joining a gaggle of foot passengers standing outside the terminal building, I watched a ship approach through the murk, before we were called forward to the pier's end as it docked. As we waited for the arriving passengers to disembark, the sound of bagpipes emanated from within the boat. A piper in Highland dress emerged and carefully negotiated the sloping gangway, playing all the while. The music reverberated across Gott Bay, moving and melancholy. The passengers parted to let the piper pass, with some of the giddier women growing hot under the collar and weak at the knees. Dress a man in a kilt and he oozes sex appeal, it seems, even if he resembles an ogre. Not that this piper was ogre-like.

We boarded, and I moved quickly through the interior of the ship and up a little flight of steps to gain the outdoor deck. A steady rain was now falling. Each of the seats had a little pool of water at their centre – a very British sight, I thought. Chivalrous men would soon be using hand-kerchiefs to mop up the wetness to ensure their wives and girlfriends had dry behinds. A dozen women, the hoods of their waterproofs drawn over their heads, stood around the deck, waving madly at the hosts who had entertained them on Tiree. The piper played on, the tune growing fainter as he progressed slowly along the pier, only for the sound to momentarily return loud and shrill, carried on the wind.

A dreich morning, twelve frantically-gesturing middle-aged women, the reflection and sadness elicited by the sound of the pipes – all parting memories of the sand, sea and sun isle of Tiree. The boat manoeuvred out of Gott Bay, its waters now grey, and set a course for the mainland. Within minutes, Tiree was gone, buried in low, swirling mist.

10

Eigg

The island of Eigg is precious.
An island is a metaphor for the world.
Together we can look after all our islands
And so take care of the world.
Isle of Eigg Heritage Trust

⚜

It was independence day, Eigg's independence day – the
13th anniversary of the day islanders became stewards of
their territory, masters of their destiny, writers of their
history. Eiggachs do not, by tradition, allow this day to
pass unnoticed. The milestone of that day of delirious
freedom was to be commemorated in obligatory Scottish
fashion – a ceilidh: an opportunity for dancing, drinking
and more delirium.

I went to Mallaig by train from Fort William, a brief yet
beautiful excursion so lauded that the route regularly ranks
in greatest-railway-journeys-in-the-world lists, raising it to
the echelon of the Trans-Siberian across Russia and the
Glacier Express in Switzerland. Yet passengers can close
their eyes as the carriages escape Fort William, a town
impaired by mystifying development and severed by a dual-
carriageway. Moscow or Zermatt, the respective starting
points of the Trans-Siberian and Glacier Express, Fort
William is not. The greyness of the Lochaber capital was
left behind by the time the train had swept over the

Caledonian Canal. And once past the factories and houses of Caol and Corpach, eyes turned to gaze across the shimmering water of Loch Eil. Incongruous beginnings, no doubt, but the 42 mile journey between Fort William and Mallaig is one of the grandest travelling experiences our country can muster.

The passage is worthy of superlatives: outstanding, supreme and unrivalled. The train passed beneath the dark roof of the nation (1344 metre Ben Nevis); overlooked the Glenfinnan monument (the memorial commemorating the occasion of Bonnie Prince Charlie raising his father's standard on a nearby hill in 1745); paused at Arisaig (Britain's most westerly train station – a marginal triumph over Kyle of Lochalsh and Mallaig); spanned the quarter-of-a-mile River Morar (reputed to be the country's shortest); and rolled by Loch Morar (our deepest lake, plunging to 310 metres), before arriving in Mallaig.

As if the natural glories of the line were not enough, Hollywood stardust is now sprinkled on the route; the 21-arch, single track Glenfinnan viaduct has featured in several Harry Potter movies. For many of the younger passengers, and indeed some of the older ones, the viaduct, standing 30 metres above ground at its highest point, was the climax of the voyage. The marvellous prospect from our lofty plinth stirred breathless gasps and squeals, with Potter fanatics dreaming they were instead onboard a steaming Hogwarts Express, a Ford Anglia giving chase.

Mallaig was bustling and excited. The port is the point of embarkation for travellers destined for Canna, Eigg, Muck and Rum, which together make up the Small Isles, and to Armadale, a village on Skye's Sleat peninsula. The talk on the pier was only of one island – Eigg. A crowd approaching 150 people, streaked with bohemians, jostled for space on the pier. I looked upon us as a privileged band; I was

imbued with a sense we were moments away from beginning an extraordinary journey to an island paradise only we
knew about, stepping temporarily into a self-ruled kingdom. We were called forward to board: fish and chips were
hurriedly finished; guitars were slung over shoulders; crates
of cider and lager were cradled. The pre-ceilidh party had
begun before the ferry's ropes had been untied. Ring pulls
being yanked on cans hissed like a chorus of pistons. The
tune of a fiddle emanated from below deck. A tattooed man,
sporting eye and nose piercings, offered me a beer. Not
wanting to appear feeble, I accepted, took a swig, and
discarded the fizzy liquid in the first bin I came to.

Eigg has every reason to celebrate. The battle for independence was hard-won and long-fought. The £274,000
purchase of Eigg by Keith Schellenberg, a Yorkshire busi-
nessman and former winter Olympian, in 1974, heralded
the beginning of two decades of uncertainty. The relationship between Schellenberg and islanders gradually deterio-
rated. Impatience grew into frustration; frustration grew
into animosity. Not long before he finally relinquished the
island, Schellenberg's vintage Rolls Royce was mysteriously
burnt out. The police investigated the fire, but the inhabitants of Eigg either did not know the arsonist or would not
reveal the identity of the perpetrator. The laird's retort was
furious, describing the small population as 'dangerous' in a
press release, before telling journalists they were 'barmy
revolutionaries' and 'rotten'. He would sell Eigg, Schellenberg confirmed – but not to a trust established by islanders
seeking a buyout.

Schellenberg kept his word, passing Eigg on to Marlin
Eckhart, a German artist known as Maruma, for £1.6
million in 1995. The trust responded by ramping up its
campaign to bring Eigg into community ownership. A bid –

£200,000 below its sale price two years earlier – was accepted, with the official handover taking place on June 12, 1997. It was a momentous occasion. Converging on Pier Hill, a commemorative plaque and a 10ft stone pillar were unveiled in front of 300 people, including residents, MPs, councillors and Highland Council dignitaries.

Adopting a Gaelic proverb, Brian Wilson, the then minister for the Highlands and islands, told the gathering: 'It is always better to light a candle than curse the darkness, and Eigg has lit a candle that would ignite a hundred more in the coming years.'

Then the party – lubricated by 90 bottles of 25-year-old Talisker whisky delivered from Skye – started, and ended three days later.

Many, many drams were raised. Recounting the first night's ceilidh, Camille Dressler, Eigg's biographer, wrote: 'As the Talisker flowed in countless toasts, the islanders, their friends and supporters danced until the small hours of the morning.'

Viewed from the sea, a cloud-free Eigg – the second largest of the Small Isles – invokes an intense physical attraction in the onlooker. The island's prominent feature is An Sgurr, a 393-metre mountain rising abrupt and sheer from squelchy moor on its south side, giving the impression of an upturned boat. The mile-long pitchstone escarpment of An Sgurr is the creation of a volcanic eruption on neighbouring Rum 58 million years ago. Slow-moving, viscous lava flowed along the path of a river, filling it to the brim, before cooling and forming columns resembling organ pipes at right angles to the valley sides. Glaciation eroded the surrounding basalt, but pitchstone lava proved a harder material, creating an inverted glen and the great prow of the Sgurr of Eigg. The geography of Eigg is almost as impressive in the north, where towering sandstone cliffs drop to the sea, while the noise made by the Singing Sands overlooking Rum have been poetically (and a little ridiculously) likened to 'the faint strains of an Aeolian harp when its strings first catch the breeze'.

As the ferry neared a pier at Galmisdale, the colourful outlines of dozens of tents became visible around the margins of the village bay. The closer to the road, and therefore Am Laimhrig – a community complex comprising a café, craft shop, grocery store and toilets – the greater the density of tents, with some shelters clumsily pitched on sloping sites. Not that it mattered. The celebrations would not conclude until after dawn, with the occupiers of the hillside tents by that time likely to be too drunk or tired to care.

This was the busiest weekend of the year, with mainland party-goers quadrupling Eigg's population of 85. The café was churning out bacon rolls and tea. Campers streamed along a coastal road in search of a pitch. The queue for the Ladies snaked out the door. Cavernous recycling bags for cans and glass outside Am Laimhrig were already filling up.

I was unsure what to do. Being a lone traveller can either be a source of formidable strength or great weakness. Compared to the camaraderie of people who were either friends or knew each other from previous anniversaries, I felt conspicuous, like a gatecrasher – a gatecrasher who was suddenly not in the party spirit. Eigg was no longer the island paradise I had envisaged. And, for a few brief moments, I was angry and resentful. I just wanted them, these island-invaders, to go away. Selfishly, I wanted Eigg to myself, like Coll and Colonsay had been. So I bought food at the store and walked away from Galmisdale to find my own place on the island.

Despite Eigg having only four-and-a-half miles of surfaced road, I managed to lose the main strip within minutes. I had got my wish; I was on my own. I was standing next to what appeared to be a pile of plastic junk. On closer inspection, the pile of plastic junk was indeed a pile of plastic junk. The detritus – predominately bottle tops and other unidentifiable plastic, all presumably washed up on the island's beaches – had been fashioned into the shape of a ground-level, giant-sized footprint. The centrepiece was a toilet brush.

Opposite was a grand building, the Earth Connections sustainability centre, according to a sign, set up with the admirable ambition to 'promote green living and inspire people to make positive changes in their lives'. Residential courses on food production, low-energy living and ways of reducing carbon footprints were due to be based here for the first time in the history of the island later that year.

A theme was emerging.

Eigg is the environmental isle of the Hebrides, a green Holy Island. The community buyout gave islanders the freedom to turn Eigg into an eco-Utopia. The energy-producing methods of old, when businesses and homes were heated by coal and oil, and electricity was generated by diesel generators, have been discarded. On-island hydro schemes, solar panels and wind turbines became the new energy suppliers, with Eigg Electric – dubbed Eigg-tricity – providing round-the-clock power for the first time in 2008.

A 10-year plan – bolstered by Eigg's success in clinching a near-third share of a £1million eco-prize in 2010 – envisaged a further strengthening of the island's green credentials: reliance on fossil fuels will be minimised; the use of fertilisers and pesticides reduced; buildings will be made more energy efficient; the majority of food will be produced on the island, with only seasonal goods imported from the mainland; the amount of waste sent to mainland landfill sites will be slashed; low-emission or electric vehicles could replace traditional vehicles.

I proceeded towards Cleadale, regaining asphalt. The road climbed gently and there was little to distract me: a church at one point, a single standing stone a short while later. I passed a house and a museum, which was once the island's post office, before the road began to drop to the west coast of Eigg. The foremost diversion was traffic – not its volume but its velocity. On the half-dozen instances that I heard the wail of an approaching vehicle, I hastily sprang from the road to avoid being flattened by the hurtling object. I seemed to have stumbled upon an island populated exclusively by rally drivers.

I found a £4 a night campsite beneath the basalt cliffs of Sgorr an Fharaidh and pitched my tent. Campsite is a generous description for the location; an area set aside for tents was made up of two wildly overgrown oblongs of grass. It was as basic as basic could be: a compost toilet, no shower, an open-air sink to wash dishes. Yet the view was astonishing, worthy of the price of a night at a five-star hotel. Across Laig Bay and the Sound of Rum, the jumbled pile of mountains that are the Rum Cuillin rose high and splendid. As I cooked and ate, a neighbouring camper played his bagpipes, the sound reverberating around the natural amphitheatre of Cleadale.

Not only was today the 13th anniversary of Eigg's community buyout, but England's first football World Cup outing, in a game against the US. I had seen a hand-written note in Galmisdale advertising a place where the football was being screened, but had neglected to write down the venue. It was a Gaelic name of something or somewhere in Cleadale, which I ignorantly assumed would be easy to find because it would surely be a pub or café. But blank faces greeted my arrival at a restaurant which I took to be the most likely contender. This was the only hostelry in Cleadale; there was no pub, no café. Then a bearded local assured me there would be no football in Cleadale.

'Have you tried Galmisdale?' he asked.

I inwardly groaned at the prospect of a three-mile walk back to Galmisdale on the off-chance that a place over-flowing with Scots on one of the biggest nights in the island's calendar would have the gall to air an England football match.

Close to giving up, I sulkily mooched towards camp, passing the sign for a bed and breakfast establishment, the name of which I recalled from the note in Galmisdale. I pushed open the door and found three men positioned around a gigantic, wide-screen television. After an initial greeting and inquiry into my nationality, and therefore my allegiance, we sat in silence. Not that we would have been able to hear one another talk, for the volume was deafening. Each house on Eigg had a maximum use limit of five kilowatts of electricity at any one time – enough to power a kettle and a washing machine. The island's wind turbines must have been spinning like crazy to power this monster of a television.

A student I had sat next to handed me a beer. There was no nearby bin to dump the contents this time around, so I drank, knowing one drink would inevitably lead to two, then three, and before I knew it, I would be playing the role of a drunken fool, toasting Eigg's independence. Jamie, a second year undergraduate studying herbal medicine, was putting his knowledge into practice by creating a herb garden on the island as part of a three-week volunteering project. His achievements were already worthy enough to gain a mention in the Eigg newsletter pinned to the notice board in Am Laimhrig. By full-time, there were 20 of us crammed into the living room – men, women, children and dogs – occupying every available inch of floor and the staircase. No-one seemed bothered by England's lacklustre draw; thoughts had turned to Galmisdale and the ceilidh.

I smartened up, which meant brushing my teeth and changing into jeans, and met Jamie at a Highland Council building he and another volunteer, Sarah, a student from Cork, were staying at during their time on the island. The three of us began the cross-island trek, weighing up the chances of us begging a lift to the community hall. Two full cars swept past, the drivers shaking apologetic heads. A third vehicle, a tatty pick-up, stopped, and the driver told us to jump in the back. Seven pairs of eyes, some more glazed than others, stared out from the rear of the vehicle. After a little jostling and shuffling, we squeezed into spaces between the revellers and the pick-up continued on its journey. A bottle of vodka, flavoured with an unidentified herb, was passed around. It was disgusting. After taking my turn to glug, I nodded at the creator of the appalling concoction, and said: 'Lovely stuff.' I felt my head swimming seconds later; it was like rocket fuel.

We roared along the road, bouncing over the bumps, the man behind the wheel another of the island's fearless rally drivers. I prayed he had not been drinking. A vivid and morose imagination was my punishment for six years as a newspaper journalist. I envisaged the driver losing control, the vehicle plunging off the road and into the sea, all of us perishing. I wish I had just walked, I thought again and again. Nor did I recall the twists and turns of the journey, a route I walked only hours earlier. It was as if we had been transported to a different island. We slowed momentarily, pausing outside Am Laimhrig, and I heard the yapping of a dog. A second later the party-spirited mongrel was among us, crawling over our legs, eagerly licking faces. The engine growled, surging up a hill, carrying the weight of 12 people.

Soon we could hear the sound of music and voices from outside, signalling our arrival at the timber-panelled community hall. The engine was cut. We disentangled limbs and jumped out one-by-one. I was relieved to escape with my life.

The ceilidh was underway. The community hall was very busy, very warm, and hotting up. We made for the bar. Events, unfortunately, became a little hazy from here on. I have a strong memory – both sight and smell – of fire, although whether it was a barbecue or an actual fire, my brain will not allow me to accurately remember. I also have a vivid recollection of brown soil emanating from the taps in the bathroom instead of water, which seemed entirely fabricated, until I was later told the occurrence was caused by a water shortage on Eigg. This much I know definitively. Early on a woman shouted her name in my ear and dragged me away to dance a reel. Soon realising that my dancing was not up to her standard, she abandoned me for a better partner. I retreated to the bar. The wonders of alcohol enabled me to dance a little more. I had another drink. Then I was properly drunk, characterised by bouts of silliness interspersed with bouts of staring vacantly into space. And then a wonderful realisation struck me: I was at the coolest party in the world, celebrating 13 years of the people's republic of Eigg, partying the night way on a Hebridean island, free-spirited and miles from anywhere.

A tent is a horrible place to hang out when hungover. And with the nearest shelter and shop an hour's walk away and rain falling in torrents, a tent, this tent, was the very worst place on the planet. I pulled the sleeping bag tightly around my shoulders, twisting my upper body in the narrow space to lie on my back, groaning aloud. My head throbbed, the beat of the ceilidh bands replaced by an angry knocking on